Barbara Marshall was born in Braunschweig/West Germany and came to England in 1966 after the completion of her *Staatsexamen* (BA/MPhil) at Munich University. She obtained a PhD in Modern History from London University in 1972 with a thesis on the political development of university towns in the Weimar Republic. Her research interests have since moved to German and British history after 1945 and most recently to European integration. She is a Senior Lecturer in European History and European Studies at the Polytechnic of North London, and lives in North London and in Suffolk with her husband and two daughters.

Other titles in the series *Makers of the Twentieth Century* in Cardinal:

de Gaulle   Julian Jackson
Deng Xiaoping   David Goodman
Martin Luther King   Adam Fairclough
Nkrumah   David Birmingham
Roosevelt   Fiona Venn

Forthcoming titles in the same series:

Trotsky   David Law
Khrushchev   Martin McCauley
Tito   Stevan K. Pavlowitch
Nehru   Denis Judd
Jinnah   Howard Brasted
Atatürk   Alan Palmer
Smuts   Iain Smith
Lenin   Beryl Williams
Adenauer   Andrew Crozier

Makers of the Twentieth Century

WILLY
Brandt

BARBARA MARSHALL

CARDINAL

A CARDINAL Book

First published in Great Britain in Cardinal by Sphere Books Ltd 1990

Typeset by Leaper & Gard Ltd, Bristol
Printed and bound in Great Britain by
Cox & Wyman Ltd, Reading

ISBN 0 7474 0501 8

Sphere Books Ltd
A Division of
Macdonald & Co (Publishers) Ltd
Orbit House
1 New Fetter Lane
London EC4A 1AR
A member of Maxwell Macmillan Pergamon Publishing Corporation

Acknowledgements

Many people helped me with this book. In Germany my thanks go to members of Willy Brandt's former and present staff, notably to Dr. K-H Klär for several interviews; to the staff of the Archive and the Library of the Friedrich-Ebert Stiftung in Bonn, to Inter Nationes for their help with German books and to Ursula Clauditz and Margot Martinsen for assistance in practical matters.

In England I am grateful to Dr. B. O'Neill for several discussions of Brandt's personality and to my husband John for his patience with the manuscript.

Contents

Editor's Foreword

The last decade of the century is a good moment to look back at some of the dominating individuals who have shaped the modern world. *Makers of the Twentieth Century* is a series of short biographical reassessments, written by specialists but aimed at a wide general audience. We hope that they will be useful to sixth-formers and students seeking a brief introduction to a new subject; but also to the ordinary reader looking for the minimum she or he needs to know of the life and legacy of the century's key figures, in a form that can be absorbed in a single sitting. At the same time we hope that the interpretations, based on the latest research – even where there is not space to display it – will be of sufficient interest to command the attention of other specialists.

The series will eventually cover all the outstanding heroes and villains of the century. They can, as a sort of party game, be sorted into three – or perhaps four – types. Some can be classed primarily as national leaders, who either restored the failing destinies of old nations (de Gaulle, Adenauer, Kemal Atatürk) or created new ones out of the collapse of the European empires (Nkrumah, Jinnah). Others were national leaders first of all, but made a still greater impact on the international stage (Franklin Roosevelt, Willy Brandt, Jan Smuts). A further category were not heads of government at all, but achieved worldwide resonance as the embodiments of powerful ideas (Trotsky and Martin Luther King). The great tyrants, however, (Hitler, Stalin, Mao Zedong) are not easily contained in any category but transcend them all.

The series, too, aims to leap categories, attempting to place each subject in a double focus, both in relation to the domestic politics of his or her own country and as an actor on the world stage – whether as builder or destroyer, role model or prophet. One consequence of the communications revolution in this century has been that the charismatic leaders of quite small countries (Castro, Ho Chi Minh, Gadaffi) can command a following well beyond the frontiers of their national constituency.

At the centre of each volume stands the individual: of course biography can be a distorting mirror, exaggerating the influence of human agency on vast impersonal events; yet unquestionably there are, as Shakespeare's Brutus observed, tides in the affairs of men 'which, taken at the flood, lead on to fortune'. At critical moments the course of history can be diverted, channelled or simply ridden by individuals who by luck, ruthlessness or destiny are able to impose their personality, for good or ill, upon their times. Who can doubt that Lenin and Hitler, Mao and Gorbachev – to name but four – have decisively, at least for a time, bent the history of our epoch to their will? These, with men and women from every major country in the world, are the *Makers of the Twentieth Century.*

John Campbell
London, 1990

Chronology

18 December 1913   Willy Brandt born in Lübeck
30 January 1933   Hitler in power in Germany
April 1933   Brandt goes into exile in Norway
1947/48   Return to Germany as press attaché of the Norwegian mission in Berlin
1948/49   Link man in Berlin between SPD in western zones and Berlin
1949–61; 1965–   SPD member of the West German parliament (*Bundestag*)
1957–66   Mayor of West Berlin
1964–87   Chairman of the SPD
1966–69   Foreign Secretary of the Federal Republic of Germany
1969–74   Chancellor of the Federal Republic of Germany
1976–   President of the Socialist International
1977–   Chairman of the North-South Commission
1987–   Honorary Chairman of the SPD (West)
1990–   Honorary Chairman of the SPD (East)

Abbreviations

APO	Extra-parliamentary opposition
CDU/CSU	Christian Democratic Union/Christian Social Union
CSCE	Conference on Security and Cooperation in Europe
DKP	Communist Party of Germany (FRG) from 1969
EEC	European Economic Community
EPC	European Political Co-operation
FDP	Free Democratic Party
FRG	Federal Republic of Germany
GDR	German Democratic Republic
IDA	International Development Agency
KPD	Communist Party of Germany 1918–33 and in the Federal Republic up to 1956
MBFR	Mutual Balanced Force Reduction
NATO	North Atlantic Treaty Organization
NPD	Neo-Nazi Party
NSDAP	National Socialist German Workers Party
SAJ	Socialist Workers Youth
SAP	Socialist Workers Party
SED	Socialist Unity Party
SI	Socialist International
SPD	Social Democratic Party of Germany

Map of Germany in relation to rest of Europe

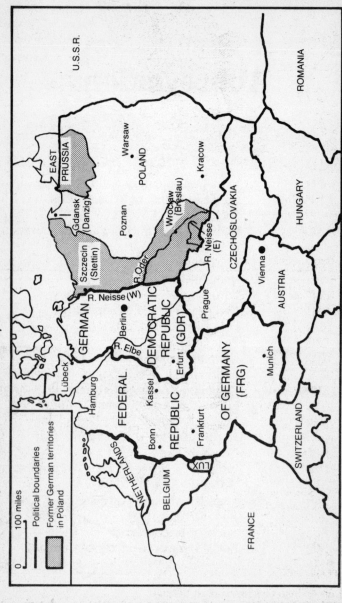

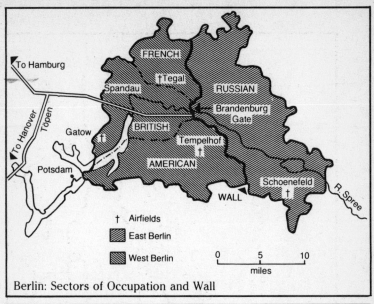

Berlin: Sectors of Occupation and Wall

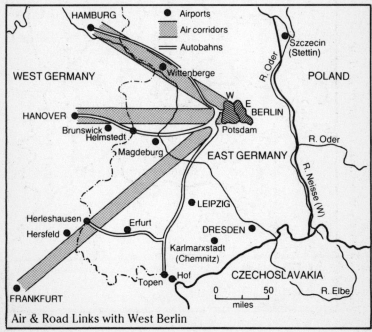

Air & Road Links with West Berlin

Introduction

The life of Willy Brandt, West Germany's first social democratic Chancellor, spans much of Germany's history in the twentieth century. The year of his birth, 1913, was the last year of Imperial Germany before the outbreak of World War I which put an end to its prosperity and predominance in Europe. The end of the war in 1918 and military defeat came as an unexpected shock for most Germans, and this was made worse by the outbreak of revolutionary upheavals which culminated in the abdication of the Kaiser on 9 November 1918. A republic was established under social democratic leadership (the 'Weimar Republic'), which was burdened from the beginning with having to sign the humiliating Peace Treaty of Versailles, with which it was henceforth associated. From 1929 Germany became one of the victims of the world economic crisis, with a third of its working population unemployed in 1932 and no long term social security net to soften the impact of misery. The republic, never really popular with the majority of Germans and paralysed by seemingly insurmountable economic and social problems, ceased to function properly after 1930. It came to an end with the appointment of Adolf

Hitler as Chancellor on 30 January 1933.

Hitler quickly established a totalitarian dictatorship, persecuting the regime's opponents, many of whom fled into exile – among them the young Willy Brandt. In 1939 Germany started the Second World War and yet again suffered defeat, which this time led to the destruction of the German nation state and its eventual division into two German states in 1949: the Federal Republic of Germany (FRG) on the territory which the three western allies (the USA, Britain and France) had occupied, and the German Democratic Republic (GDR) in the former Soviet Zone. The two states were caught up in the emerging Cold War between the USA and the Soviet Union, with the FRG eventually integrated in the western 'bloc' through membership in NATO (North Atlantic Treaty Organization) and the EEC (European Economic Community), and the GDR into the equivalent Warsaw Pact and Comecon (1955).

The policy of western integration was pursued in West Germany by the first conservative Chancellor Konrad Adenauer (CDU, 1949–63); he also followed a course of strict non-recognition of the GDR as a state and applied the Hallstein Doctrine to deter other states from doing so: every country which established diplomatic links with the GDR would forfeit those with the FRG. Under Adenauer the country experienced a period of reconstruction, of political stability and of economic growth. His successor Ludwig Erhard (CDU, 1963–6), although the father of the 'economic miracle', fell over a slight economic crisis and was replaced in 1966 by the Grand Coalition under Kurt Georg Kiesinger (CDU, 1966–9) between CDU and SPD, in which Brandt became Foreign Secretary. In foreign policy a cautious course of reappraisal was followed in line with the general reorientation in the relations among the superpowers after the Cuban missile crisis. Internally the later 1960s were marked by widespread youth protests (not only in Germany) and demands for reform; a section

2

of this protest movement deteriorated into groups of urban terrorists which confronted successive German governments with the problem of law and order. Brandt's government (SPD, 1969–74) tackled both demands and in foreign policy carried out a new initiative, the so-called *Ostpolitik*: the opening of West Germany to the east and the gradual increase in her freedom of action in international affairs. Brandt's successor, Helmut Schmidt (SPD, 1974–82) continued these policies which were made more difficult by the rise in energy prices (the 'oil crisis', 1973). Under Schmidt the FRG was better able to cope with these developments than other comparable countries and emerged at the beginning of the 1980s as a prosperous, modern state. It played an increasingly independent international role, particularly when in the period of the new 'freeze' in the relations among the superpowers détente in Europe seemed to be threatened, affecting both German states directly because they constituted the front line of their respective 'blocs'. Chancellor Helmut Kohl (CDU, 1982 to the present) pursued more conservative internal policies in response to a new economic crisis, and in foreign affairs sought to adjust more to the position of the USA. The coming to power of Gorbachev in the USSR in 1985 brought with it the application of *glasnost* to Eastern Europe and to East Germany which led to enormous changes and the unification of the two German states in the near future.

The life and political development of Willy Brandt reflects these events and illustrates some of the fundamental problems which the Germans have faced in their recent history. There was the experience of the defeat of the Left (and other democrats) by Hitler's takeover of power, followed by the experience of exile, which for many was vital for their physical survival. However, after the war this raised tensions between those who had survived in hardship inside Germany and those who had passed the time in relative comfort abroad. Brandt encapsulates this dilemma particularly well, not only because of the way he lived in Norway during the Third Reich but also in the reactions to him, the former emigré, when he stood as candidate for Chancellor in the 1961 and 1965 elections. Emigrés raised the uncomfortable issue of what constituted a 'good' German, the question of a German identity.

This was posed in a different way when Brandt was Foreign Secretary and Chancellor. The international wave of student unrest produced in Germany for the first time open questions about National Socialism, and the desire of the younger generation for a more open, modern society was taken up in Germany by the Brandt government. Brandt's *Ostpolitik* confronted the Germans with the reality of their military defeat in 1945 which had created boundaries and new realities which needed to be respected.

The oil crisis of the 1970s brought with it the questioning of growth and the necessity of setting priorities. Growing concern for environmental problems and the ever increasing needs of the Third World were worldwide problems which required global responses for their solution. Again Brandt illustrates this new awareness with his work on the North–South Commission.

Lastly, Brandt reflects the dilemma over German unification: enthusiasm for a single German nation is coupled with awareness of the problems created by a new unified nation state in the centre of Europe and the anxieties of Germany's neighbours.

The Early Years, 1913–45

1

YOUTH (1913–33)

The town of Lübeck in which Willy Brandt was born on 18 December 1913 was a wealthy city which owed much of its prosperity to its port on the Baltic Sea. It had been a member of the Hansa League, and its leading patrician class was characterized by centuries of world-wide trading links which had instilled the seemingly quiet confidence which the novelist Thomas Mann depicts so well in *Buddenbrooks*. For the town this meant excellent cultural and educational provision from which the young Willy Brandt was later to benefit greatly. However, there was another side to the city; a poor working class which prided itself on its own traditions and culture. Between the two there was little contact.

Brandt was born Herbert Ernst Karl Frahm, the illegitimate son of a nineteen-year-old sales assistant; he adopted his present name only later when he was forced to hide his true identity after Hitler had come to power in Germany. He belonged thus to the other, the poor Germany. His grandfather in his youth had been a labourer on a landed estate in Mecklenburg where he was still treated like a bondsman with corporal punishment for a slight offence. He had revolted and eventually moved to Lübeck where he became a factory worker and later the driver of a factory lorry. His grandfather was to some extent typical of the rising, self-improving working class of the early twentieth century with a small library in which August Bebel's *Women and Sexuality* had a prominent place. Brandt's mother showed the same characteristics. She tried to speak proper German (as against the local dialect, 'Platt', normally used in working class circles). She was an avid reader with books regularly borrowed from the co-op library; she belonged to the workers' dramatic society and had an annual subscription to the local 'People's Theatre' where the German classics were regularly performed, although Schiller more than Goethe because he was more revolutionary. Brandt's mother could recite long passages by heart. When Brandt was born his mother had to continue to work and therefore left him in the care of a neighbour. Brandt remembers having been a lonely child, left to himself for many hours and without many playmates.[1]

His mother and grandfather never mentioned his father's name. Brandt, according to his latest Memoirs, only dared to make enquiries much later, after the war: he was John Möller, a clerk in a firm in Hamburg who died in 1958 without ever having shown any interest in his son. Möller apparently had the reputation of having been exceptionally gifted with the wish to become a schoolmaster. To those who knew him he had been an 'impressive personality'.

Up to the age of five Brandt was brought up exclusively by women, until his life changed when his grandfather returned from World War I in 1918. Brandt called him papa immediately and formed a deep attachment to him (although he later discovered that he was not even his real grandfather). It was therefore not surprising that when his widowed grandfather remarried in 1919 Brandt showed intense jealousy of his 'step-grandmother', called her aunt and remained aloof from her. Brandt lived with them and now saw his mother only twice a week. She did not seem to show much closer interest in him although she loved dressing him up in smart clothes; pictures survive showing a pretty child in an array of different outfits, such as the uniform of a soldier of the Wilhelmine army or a sailor's uniform.

Brandt was a very bright boy, easily the best in his class, who loved reading and at thirteen he won a scholarship to the Johanneum, a local grammar school of great reputation. The four years spent at the Johanneum were decisive for his intellectual development, and Brandt recalls particularly the German and History teacher who through informal discussions was always stimulating, provoking contradiction and debate. The open-mindedness of the staff was illustrated by the fact that during his final year he was allowed to write an extended essay about the former Social Democrat leader August Bebel – grammar schools in the Weimar Republic were normally notoriously nationalist and 'anti-left'. His English teacher for example was worried by Brandt's left political activities; he warned his mother that 'the boy is gifted – what a pity, politics will ruin him.'

The Johanneum was important to the young Brandt not only because of the excellent education but because for the first time he met middle and upper class boys and teachers who were unsympathetic to the republic. Brandt on the other hand had been born into the working class and into socialism: his mother (and later her husband) and grandfather were active members of the SPD and the Trade Unions; they were deeply committed to the Weimar Republic which had brought the eight hour working day and the vote to women. From it they hoped for further improvements, although his grandfather was always aware of the threats to the system, that one day it might be swept away. From the beginning the young

Brandt was immersed in working class culture. He joined the children's (boys' and girls') groups of the workers' sports association, such as the *Kinderfreunde*, and later the Red Falcons (boy scouts). He loved the romanticism of camp life – the hiking and singing by the camp fire; the nightly debates on the meaning of life. He was a good swimmer, but no athlete: he won a 5000 m race only because he was the only contestant. Camp life taught lessons in practical democracy and voluntary discipline which he was keen to enforce: he voted for the exclusion from the group of boys who had been caught smoking. Moreover, the group which he led voted in favour of having only boys as members. The camaraderie of the group became for Brandt an *ersatz* for the family he had lacked. He was well liked because of his sense of fun, but, as he recalled later, 'I had many friends but no one who was really close to me. I felt it difficult to confide in other people. From my early years I had maintained this reserve; accustomed to live within myself I found it not easy to share my sentiments and inner thoughts with others. I was popular but as far as I was concerned, my relations with schoolmates remained superficial ...' He had a gift for organization and was a good speaker. From this early age his life centred on involvement in politics. In 1929 he moved on to the Socialist Workers Youth (SAJ) and for a time was deputy chairman of the district Lübeck/Mecklenburg. In recognition of his outstanding potential he became a full member of the SPD in 1930 at the age of only sixteen – the minimum age was normally eighteen.

Brandt had grown into a handsome young man who was highly attractive to girls: tall with thick, wavy hair, soft eyes and dimples in his cheeks when he laughed. At this early age he was already contributing editor of the local Social Democrat daily, the *Volksbote*. He had written frequent contributions to the paper from the age of fourteen and had decided to become a journalist. At the

Volksbote he met the man who was to have a decisive influence on him: the editor in chief Julius Leber. (He was murdered by the Nazis in January 1945 for his involvement in the 20 July 1944 plot to kill Hitler). What impressed Brandt was that Leber was an intellectual who at the same time could speak for the man in the street – a quality which he himself was to display later with great effect. His conflicts with party bureaucrats ('stifling the creative energies of youth', 'captives of outdated formulas and slogans',) made him particularly popular with a rebellious young man such as Brandt. Leber became a father figure for him. According to Brandt's own account Leber dispelled his latent self doubts by giving him recognition and encouragement. 'His occasional praise meant all the more to me because he also never hesitated to criticize my youthful impetuosity.' His main and very effective weapon was irony. But most important for the young Brandt was that 'he treated me as his equal; he took me seriously....'

On the other hand the SAJ and Brandt in it were on the left of the party which criticized Leber on a number of issues. In the early 1930s, the period of world economic crisis, mass unemployment and political radicalization, the debate within the Lübeck SPD illustrates the dilemma of the SPD at national level at that time. There were many areas of conflict, of which the question of how to confront National Socialism was the most divisive. Leber and the SPD leadership favoured a wait and see approach on the assumption that National Socialism was a product of the economic crisis and would collapse as soon as the economic situation improved. The main thing for them was to have the SPD organization survive intact for the day when the party would resume power. The left on the other hand was determined to fight fascism here and now, seeing in it the fundamental threat of capitalism in its most aggressive form. Brandt was typical of the young on the left: they got involved in street fights with the Hitler Youth and expressed more and more violent criticism of the SPD leadership, particularly after the September elections of 1930 which made the NSDAP into the second largest parliamentary party after the SPD.

In frequent debates with Leber the young Brandt defined his position as a radical follower of the left: social reforms were 'sedatives to paralyse the activity and energy of the masses'; socialism was more important than the republic. The break with his mentor became inevitable. On the other hand Brandt experienced at the same time a quite different political scene when, in the summer of 1931 he went on a trip to Norway. He was not only impressed by the natural beauty of the country and the calm dignity of its people. He also had a first meeting with Scandinavian style social democracy.

When in early October 1931 two left wing members of the SPD who had been expelled from the party set up a new organization, the SAP (*Sozialistische Arbeiterpartei*), Brandt and about half of the Socialist Youth organization with him, joined enthusiastically. In order to prevent the further drift of the socialist youth into the SAP, Leber called a meeting in October which the left with their 'Shouting Guard' tried to disrupt. There were scuffles and fighting broke out; the pupil Frahm was mentioned as one of the leaders of the wild heap of 'splitters'. Leber's attempts to persuade Brandt that the SAP was condemned to remain a small group of sectarians, were in vain, particularly the avuncular approach: 'In spite of your youth you can appreciate a good book, a good drink, the favours of a beautiful girl. You are quite normal, you don't belong with that band of sectarians'.

Leber was right in his assessment: the SAP never gained the support of substantial elements among the older members of the SPD; its election results remained poor (0.2 per cent in July 1932). For Brandt personally SAP membership and the break with Leber had drastic consequences: he lost his job at the *Volksbote* and also the financial support for his future university studies which Leber had promised. As all his work for the SAP was honorary he joined a firm of shipping brokers after his Abitur in the autumn of 1932. It was unexciting work but provided him with useful contacts with sailors, fishermen and Scandinavian clients.

Brandt, as leader of the SAP's Youth Section, was automatically a member of the SAP executive committee. He worked immensely hard as an instructor, organizer and speaker for the new party. He would cycle the 60 km from Lübeck to Hamburg to get prominent speakers to come to Lübeck. In this way the SAP's national leaders came to Lübeck. Brandt made such an impression that he was invited to stand as the party's candidate at the next diet elections. Nobody was aware that he had not yet reached the minimum age.

For anti-fascist activists such as Brandt the coup by the central German government on 20 July 1932 against Prussia was a decisive event. Recent Prussian elections had not produced a workable majority and the Social Democrats there continued to run the state in a caretaker capacity. However, as they were politically out of step with the national government, the latter, in breach of the constitution, simply dismissed the Prussians. In this situation the response of the SPD leadership, to take the national government to court but not to oppose it more forcefully in the streets (civil war with a massive bloodbath might have ensued with victory for the left uncertain), appeared particularly feeble. Brandt recalls how 'all Prussia seethed with indignation' about their betrayal of the ordinary party members many of whom were prepared and ready to fight. Almost thirty years after the event Brandt's memoirs, the style of which is generally rather restrained, recall the emotions vividly: 'To be defeated in a battle, heroically fought against tremendous odds, is tragic; to surrender without a fight makes a tragedy a farce. It robs the victim of his last, most precious possession: his self respect....'

How limited the powers of the left had become once Hitler had actually come to power was shown in the way in which it was not possible even to free Julius Leber who had been arrested on the night of 30 January 1933, the day of Hitler's appointment as German Chancellor. When Leber was arrested the Lübeck workers were highly incensed and there were demands for a general strike. Brandt was a member of a delegation to the chairman of the local branch of the trade union organization (ADGB). The latter refused even to read the strike resolution. 'Did we not know that according to the latest decrees strikes were strictly forbidden, against the law?' By this time Hitler represented the legal government of Germany and opposing his decrees was an unlawful act. The dilemma of the moderate left in Germany was yet again evident.

In March 1933 Brandt attended a clandestine meeting of the by now illegal SAP in Dresden; in order to disguise his identity Brandt used a different name: Herbert Frahm became 'Willy Brandt'. (The origin of the pseudonym is not clear). This party conference had important consequences for the SAP and for Brandt personally. It was decided to build up a network of headquarters abroad, such as Paris and Oslo, for which delegates were chosen who were particularly endangered in Germany because of their previous political exposure. Brandt did not play a prominent role at Dresden but he was greatly impressed by the former communists he met, such as the writer Paul Fröhlich who had been chosen as SAP representative in Oslo; Brandt was given the task of preparing his trip to Norway from the Baltic coast. However, before Fröhlich could set out on the journey he was arrested and Brandt was chosen to go to Oslo instead; as Fröhlich would be subjected to harsh interrogation Brandt's safety was immediately at risk, although in the event Fröhlich did not give anything away. For the nineteen year old

Brandt this was a unique chance: he was given an important task abroad for his party in a country which he had learned to love and away from a Germany in which defeats for the left, persecution of Jews and other opponents of the regime, had become a daily occurrence. Moreover, particularly after Fröhlich's arrest it was only a question of time before Brandt would be caught too. He had received warnings that the police were already searching for him for the illegal distribution of leaflets. When on 1 April the first anti-semitic violence took place in Lübeck, his decision was made quickly. He left on one of the following days, although the precise date is not certain. There was little in his private life to hold him, particularly as his then girl friend Gertrude promised to follow as soon as possible. Two years later, on 14 June 1935, his beloved grandfather committed suicide, unable to cope with the distress of cancer of the stomach and of the political situation in Germany. Brandt had lost his most personal link with his native town.

It is perhaps significant that looking back to his youth Brandt later describes it in almost impersonal terms. 'Of the boy Herbert Frahm, of his first fourteen years, I have only an unclear memory. An unpenetrable veil hangs over those years, grey as the fog over the Lübeck harbour....' At fourteen began his rise from his humble beginnings; the attendance at a prestigious school gave him the decisive chance. Before that age lay his illegitimate birth, his lack of a family and his poverty which he was determined to leave behind.

EXILE (1933–45)

When he left Lübeck Brandt was convinced that he would return within two years by which time National Socialism would have been defeated by the problems of the economic situation. His clandestine journey took him from

Travemunde via Rodbyhavn to Copenhagen and was, according to Brandt 'the worst journey of my life'. From there he went on to Oslo. The reason why Norway had been chosen by the SAP for one of its centres abroad was the close ideological proximity with the Norwegian Labour Party. The latter adhered to a revolutionary Marxism but had rejected the leadership of Moscow. This affinity between the two parties led to substantial support for the SAP in Norway: already in March 1933 the Norwegian party began to collect money for persecuted German colleagues and, what was more important, through intercession with the police for foreigners they succeeded in preventing political emigrés such as Brandt from simply being moved on across the next border as undesirable aliens. Only two years later was Brandt definitely safe, when the Labour Party took over power from the previous bourgeois/conservative regime in March 1935. The new government followed a more liberal course towards refugees.

According to his own account Brandt left Germany with a briefcase with some shirts, the first volume of Marx's *Das Kapital* and 100 RM. On arrival in Oslo he made contact with the Labour Party's press bureau as instructed by the SAP. Fin Moe, the influential foreign editor of the *Arbeiderbladet* (Workers Paper) helped Brandt to obtain a job in the secretariat as well as a small monthly allowance out of a special party fund. However, only a few months later Brandt had learnt enough Norwegian to be financially independent – giving German lessons, interpreting and writing a great number of articles for different newspapers but mainly for *Arbeiderbladet* where he wrote under a number of pseudonyms mainly about the anti-fascist struggle, conditions in Germany and day-to-day politics. He and other contributors who were also political emigrés did much to preserve the image of the 'other', the non-Nazi Germany in the Norwegian public's mind. Compared to his poverty in Lübeck his standard of living rose. He was able to rent a small flat with his girl friend who had obtained her resident permit through a 'paper marriage' to a Norwegian student. This relative prosperity was rare in ordinary emigré circles. Brandt was fortunate in the help he received from the Norwegian Labour Party and in his ability as a young man to learn and to make the best of the given circumstances. As chairman of the Oslo Refugee Federation he had a good insight into the problems and weaknesses of refugees who lacked his adaptability. He did not want to remain an outsider like them. He loved Oslo because it was compact, provincial and yet cosmopolitan. There was none of the feeling of oppression which he later felt in bigger cities.

Politically the years in Norway had a decisive influence: he developed from a radical, sectarian position to that of a pragmatic democratic socialism. His initial immaturity showed in the way in which he got involved in Norwegian politics, and in particular in the Norwegian Labour Party, where after an initial period of timidity he became an active and, in the eyes of some, 'at times a rebellious'[2] member of the Socialist Youth which was linked to the Labour Party. With time he lost a part of what Brandt admits had been 'my exaggerated self-confidence', 'but not my critical outlook'. He got involved in the internal conflicts between the main party and the Youth organization, and succumbed to the (in his own words) 'arrogant' temptation to 'convey lessons from the German defeat'. There was particular irritation in the Labour Party when he joined the left wing *Mot Dag* (Towards a New Day). For Brandt this was a stimulating experience in terms of literary discoveries, the broadening of intellectual horizons and contacts with leading writers and artists, but politically he soon became disillusioned when *Mot Dag* did not want to work within the Labour Party (which was now in power). To his surprise his political extremism did not lead to a break in the continued personal support he received from important members of the Labour Party who, Brandt recalls gratefully, did not exclude him from the party which would have hardened his political arrogance, brought material difficulties and ultimately would have led to his expulsion from the country. On the contrary the leader of the party, Oscar Torp, was particularly active on his behalf, intervening with the police and persuading him to register as a student at Oslo university as a cover activity. Although he followed lectures on history and passed a preliminary examination in philosophy he was not really serious about his studies, lacking time and patience for a real commitment. One lasting result of his time at the university was his collaboration in a translation into Norwegian of Karl Marx's *Das Kapital*.

Brandt had gone to Norway to work for the SAP and political work remained an all absorbing, ceaseless activity. It involved the writing of pamphlets and the collection of money which was sent to Paris and then given out to the dependants of the politically persecuted. Sometimes it was possible to do more, as in the case of the mobilization of Norwegian judges in support of SAP accused on trial in Berlin, which so impressed their Nazi colleagues that the SAP accused got off with relatively light sentences. Brandt was also involved in the campaign to obtain the 1936 Nobel Peace Prize for the well known German publicist and campaigner Carl von Ossietzky, who as editor of the weekly journal *Weltbühne* since before World War I had been a biting critic of the German establishment, which had led to his imprisonment before and after 1933. The international campaign to reward his activities was successful but he was not able to accept the award in person.

Meanwhile Brandt's work for the SAP continued. He was chairman of the Oslo Office and had also been put in charge of the Central Office Abroad of the party's youth section. He worked in comparative isolation from older, more experienced party leaders and this led to complaints that the young Brandt was behaving like a 'mini-dictator'[3]. As time went on he became more controversial in his party and among emigrés generally which was partly due also to the obvious contradictions in his political position. On the one hand he became greatly impressed by the more moderate stance of the Norwegian Labour Party. (To the consternation of the SAP leadership Brandt published a positive article in the SAP journal.) On the other hand in relation to Germany he remained committed to a revolutionary socialism.

From Oslo he participated in the setting up of a new revolutionary Youth International. In order to prepare this twelve independent youth groups arranged to meet in Laaren in Holland in February 1934, but this meeting was broken up by the police. Although four Germans were arrested Brandt escaped because he had Norwegian identity papers. The remaining participants reconvened in Brussels where the International was set up.

His travels abroad were particularly frequent between 1936 and 1938 when the SAP and the SAJ were actively involved in the formation of a German Popular Front in exile. However, this did not come about because the political divisions among the different groups were insurmountable and the suspicion remained that the communists were using the good will of the others for their own purposes. For Brandt these travels had been fascinating opportunities to meet some of the most outstanding political and intellectual figures of his time. Moreover, the fact that his signature was included in a number of international appeals for the setting up of a German People's Front, demonstrates the importance which Brandt had gained by this stage: the signatures were a kind of 'Who's Who' of the German elites in exile.

For this reason he was chosen to go to Berlin in the summer of 1936 to carry out 'Organization Metro', to rebuild the party organization there which had been decimated by Gestapo arrests. He travelled as a student from Oslo and this cover was no hardship for Brandt, it gave him an opportunity to sit in the library every morning and to read widely, including Hitler's *Mein Kampf.* Nevertheless the stress of living undercover remained; all the more so as Berlin was awash with swastikas, with some even in working class areas. The latter came as a particularly painful surprise, as while in Paris Brandt had signed declarations of the People's Front which spoke of the 'deep and common longing of almost all Germans for an end of the terror and the restitution of human rights'.

Despite the satisfactory completion of his Berlin mission and his work in Oslo, Brandt was not elected to the SAP's executive committee at a meeting in Czechoslovakia at the end of 1936. 'The time of the twenty three year old had not yet come'[4], although it was a mark of his self esteem that he even thought this a possibility. The lasting impression which Brandt took from the conference was the level of disagreement and the futile arguments among the delegates, which revealed the frustrations of a group of political activists condemned to impotence.

One decision taken at the conference was to send Brandt on a fact finding mission to Spain where since July 1936 the right wing forces of General Franco had been trying to overthrow the legal Republican government. Brandt went to Barcelona in February 1937 officially to act as liaison between SAP members on the Aragon Front and the POUM [Trotskyist] militia. The time there was for Brandt 'full of the most contradictory impressions and of important experiences which later largely determined my political actions and thinking'; the events to him seemed cruel and confused. There was the naivety and political ignorance of many revolutionary leaders. Above all the communists' power game in the midst of the overriding struggle of the combined left against Franco's forces was deeply disillusioning. Spain gave Brandt – and many political activists of his generation – first hand experience of Stalin's political strategies.

By the time World War II broke out Brandt's travels and contacts abroad had taught him lasting political lessons. The lack of realism of many political leaders when faced with dictatorship, revolution and civil war was depressing. This was in marked contrast to the programme of social reforms and economic planning which the Scandinavian Labour Parties tried to realize and for which they also gained the support of a large segment of the middle classes and of the farming population. 'I had overcome my original left-socialist position, not its revolutionary elan, but its dogmatic narrowness ... Thus I became a Social Democrat of the Scandinavian type.' Not surprisingly his conversion to political pragmatism led to controversy with his erstwhile SAP colleagues who claimed that firm principles were not Brandt's strength.

On 5 September 1938 the German government had deprived Brandt of his German nationality, this was common practice in cases of proven 'anti-German' activities by emigrés. Considering Brandt's political engagement it had taken the German authorities unusually long to take this measure. The reason may be that for some time they remained unaware of Brandt's true identity; all official reports listed him still as 'Frahm'. With the loss of his German citizenship Brandt became stateless which did not affect him as long as he remained inside Norway and under the protection of the Norwegian government. However, Brandt was particularly endangered by the German occupation in April 1940. If caught without valid identification he could be shot on the spot. He therefore tried to escape to Sweden in May 1940 but found his route blocked by German forces. The best disguise in this situation seemed to be a Norwegian uniform which friends provided; he would be inconspicuous among thousands of other Norwegian soldiers. He was taken prisoner at the beginning of June but soon sent 'home' to Oslo. He spent weeks in hiding in a country hut provided by friends but it was a period of uncertainty and depression. Eventually he escaped to Sweden which for him meant going into exile for the second time, as the Norwegian government in exile had just approved his Norwegian citizenship. Sweden was not particularly welcoming to a new flood of political refugees as it was anxious to preserve its neutrality. Brandt faced anxious moments with internment by the police from which he had to be bailed out by a member of the Swedish *Riksdag*. As previously in Oslo he soon made a living with his usual journalistic activity.

Shortly before Christmas 1940 he secretly returned to Oslo and witnessed the impressive stance of the Norwegian people towards the German occupation; all supreme judges had just resigned in protest against decrees issued by the German *Reichskommissar* which in their view violated Norwegian law and 90 per cent of teachers refused to expound 'actively and positively' the ideas of Nazism in Norwegian schools.

Back in Stockholm he had no more problems with the Swedish authorities and he came into contact with a far wider circle not only of leading Swedish literary, political and trade union leaders but also of prominent socialists from other European countries. This 'Little Socialist International' met for the first time on 2 July 1942 at the invitation of a Norwegian, and from then on there were regular meetings at which the problems of the future of Europe and of Germany were debated intensively. Brandt was elected honorary secretary. By this stage his political analyses of the international situation and his ideas for a possible post-war order in Europe had won him widespread recognition. Bruno Kreisky, the former Austrian Chancellor, in exile in Stockholm at the time, remembers Brandt as 'political intelligence personified and above all a man of leader capacity. Willy Brandt became the

representative figure of the German speaking emigrés.'[5]
This prominence might explain the particular virulence with
which his national reliability was put into doubt – a
problem which in different guises was to dog Brandt's
later political career. It was the seeming conflict between
his German past and his newly acquired Norwegian
identity which to more hostile observers was irreconcilable. To German emigrés he was too Norwegian and to
the others too German, particularly as he defended the
Germans against the diatribes of Lord Vansittart who in a
series of broadcasts in the BBC ('Black Record': Germans
Past and Present) was putting forward the idea that *all*
Germans were contaminated with the evil spirit of
National Socialism. The link was that for Brandt commitment to anti-fascism was greater than his attachment to
either the German or the Norwegian nation state. His
loathing for National Socialism was such that, unlike
many emigrés, he never doubted the truth of reports of
the concentration camps.

The 'Little International' made its first task to work out
'Peace Aims of Democratic Socialists'. Brandt as secretary
was charged with drafting the group's foreign policy
principles. How far he was still thinking from a German
point of view is illustrated by a controversy between him
and Kreisky, when in a preliminary discussion the
Austrian flatly refused to accept Brandt's statement that
after the war Germany and Austria should remain united,
as this, according to Brandt, had been the desire of both
countries ever since the end of World War I, there must
be an end to the old division of Europe into small states.
Kreisky, the greater realist, insisted that, after the igno-
minious *Anschluss* to Nazi Germany, Austria must become
an independent state again.

Members of the International had access to the international press and followed military and political developments closely. However, a formulation of the Peace Aims
was so complex that it took the International almost a

year to come to some conclusions, these Brandt was able to reveal on 1 May 1943 at a public meeting in a Stockholm restaurant. It was an important event with several hundred participants from fourteen nations. Brandt took as his main theme that the war could be won militarily but lost politically. Peace with the Germans should be concluded on the basis of the Atlantic Charter of August 1941, which demanded the right to self determination for all nations. Although Germany had started the war the German people were not *all* guilty of having caused the war. The Nazis, together with their conservative and bourgeois-capitalist helpers were guilty, whereas the German anti-fascists were innocent, although all Germans were responsible for what had been done in their name. All Germans had to accept the consequences of the Third Reich; Jews and others persecuted by the regime were to be compensated as a matter of honour (*Ehrensache*). Most difficult was the debate over Germany's future borders and her sovereignty. This Brandt tried to circumvent with the idea of a future European Integration in which Germany would play the role of a second rate power. It would abandon all plans for hegemony and attempt by a genuine, active peace policy within the European community of nations, to win back the lost trust. It should aim at a *rapprochement* between east and west and not tie itself to one of the big powers. The Allies' war-time alliance should be continued and an all embracing League of Nations should mediate, below which regional trade, commercial, customs or currency arrangements should cement regional cooperation.

Brandt further developed these ideas in a brochure *After Victory – the Discussion of War and Peace Aims*. From the press he had learnt that the big powers intended to move Poland's borders westwards to the Oder-Neisse line. To him this was the exact replica of German expansionist policies. He conceded secretly that East Prussia with its capital Konigsberg might fall to

Poland (this caused him problems with refugees later), but the general answer for him was more flexible border arrangements. There should be a common Basic Law for the United Nations of Europe which should give all Europeans equal rights so that their security would not have to be fought for in wars with each other. These ideas were later to become the basis of Brandt's *Ostpolitik*.

Brandt's socialist credentials emerged most clearly when he discussed the future shape of German society. Like many emigrés he expected 'the rising of the broad masses at the end of the war'. Germany would be changed by a social revolution, so that Fascism would be eradicated once and for all and the survival of a radical democratic and socialist republic would be guaranteed. As a response to the division of the labour movement during the Weimar Republic, which many held responsible for the defeat of the Left, Brandt like many other members of the Left, demanded a united trade union (*Einheitsgewerkschaft*) and a united party of the Left which would link with all progressive forces to secure and underpin the democratic revolution.

While in Brandt's opinion it was important that the Germans themselves should bring about political changes in their country, he realized early on that the USA would remain in Europe and that the Americans would play a key role in Germany's future. In 1944 he approached the US Embassy in Stockholm with his ideas. These were received with interest and throughout the year 1944 the embassy sent a series of secret reports about them to Washington. On 22 May a personal assessment of Brandt was included 'Brandt is a young but obviously thoughtful and serious observer of the German scene.'[6] It was very likely that, despite his Norwegian nationality, he would play a significant role after the war.

Brandt's growing political stature was also reflected in the fact that he was approached by an emissary of the German resistance movement about whether he would be prepared to take on a post in a government after the overthrow of Hitler. His former mentor Julius Leber had become involved with the movement which culminated in the abortive coup of the 20 July 1944 and sent word to Brandt via this intermediary. For the time being he was to remain in Scandinavia; Brandt agreed although his commitment was never put into practice.

It was on 1 May 1945 in the course of a meeting of the International that Brandt received the news that Hitler had committed suicide. The meeting listened to it in stunned silence. No-one seemed to be able to believe that the atrocities and sufferings had really come to such an end. For Brandt the end of the war brought agonising decisions about his own future. His job, to collect information about Norway under occupation and about Germany had come to an end. He needed full-time employment but had to decide first whether to stay in Norway or to return to Germany.

He had spent decisive formative years in Norway and had emerged 'sound in body and mind'. Moreover, he had won recognition as a politician, having shed his more revolutionary leanings. His ideas for the future of Europe and of Germany were taken seriously. As a person he had matured, particularly after the failure of his first marriage. He had met Carlota Thorkildsen, the daughter of a Norwegian engineer, at Oslo university several years earlier, she was nine years older than Brandt but they were married on 30 June 1941. (His former girl friend Gertrude had finally left him and gone to New York as the assistant of the psychoanalyst Wilhelm Reich.) The couple moved in with her parents and when the German army invaded Norway on 9 April 1940 Carlota was pregnant; a daughter, Nina, was born in October 1940. According to his own account Brandt loved the family life; this of course he had missed in his own childhood and the need of a mother figure could be detected in the unusual age difference between the partners. For these reasons alone it was not surprising that the marriage did not work; Carlota left Brandt in January 1943. There were other contributory factors such as other women and the disruption of family life because of Brandt's escape to Sweden, although Carlota had followed him there in the spring of 1941. Brandt's intense political engagement also posed problems, particularly when the defeat of Germany became imminent and his commitment to Germany proved stronger than that to Norway.

Exile had not only been an education, the international travels had been exciting and fun. There had been adventure and love. His *joie de vivre* comes through well in his description of Paris in the late 1930s. With a Norwegian friend he came across a restaurant which advertised *Fromage à discretion avec vin – 20 francs*. After they had eaten twenty different varieties of cheese and drunk a copious amount of wine they asked for more. The owner threw them out. There had been little enough opportunity for such indulgence during the war years, but Brandt's appetite for life remained undiminished.

Brandt in Berlin, 1946-66

2

RETURN TO GERMANY (1945-8)

The end of the war in May 1945 had left most German cities in ruins, without basic services or transportation and it became the priority of the Allies occupying the country to get these going again, so as to avoid the outbreak of serious disease. An attempt to settle Germany's political and economic future was only made at the Potsdam Conference (July/August 1945) which endorsed earlier war-time decisions to divide the country into four zones of military occupation. A future central German administration (which never materialized owing to disagreements among the Allies) was to be controlled by an inter-allied Control Commission. Germany was to be treated as an economic unit; this was to enable all Allies to take reparations from the whole country. In recognition of the devastation of their country the Soviets were to receive most, for which the resources of their zone were inadequate. The position of Berlin remained an anomaly, it was situated in the middle of the Soviet Zone but divided into four sectors. The independence of, and the link between, the three western sectors and the Federal Republic remained a major problem; the city's obvious vulnerability to Soviet pressure in times of an escalating East-West confrontation gave it crucial importance.

With the war over, Brandt continued to work as a journalist in both Norway and Sweden. A possible return to Germany was not easy because the western Allies, fearful of the overcrowding in the bombed out cities and of undesirably radical elements coming back to make trouble, made entry into their zone conditional on the availability of a job and accommodation, and even then an applicant often faced long delays. An opportunity came earlier than expected for Brandt when in October 1945 he was sent as a reporter for the Norwegian Social Democratic Party newspaper to report on the Nuremberg Trials. On his way there he was able to visit his mother, stepfather and brother and old friends. He was profoundly shaken by the physical condition of the cities and by the political and moral apathy of the German people. Years of commitment to National Socialism and a most destructive war had left the Germans exhausted and preoccupied mainly with physical survival. It became all too obvious how far from reality had been his expectations of a revolutionary upsurge which would have swept away the remnants of National Socialism.

Brandt was also deeply disappointed politically. Far from relying on anti-fascists for the reconstruction of the country and the purge of National Socialism the Allies treated all Germans with equal suspicion. In particular it was the blanket ban on political activities, imposed on 2 June 1945, which impeded all political activists, but particularly the German Left at a time when, with National Socialism discredited by the country's military defeat and destruction, there would have been a great measure of support for their objectives. Instead there was the non-fraternization rule which forbade allied soldiers to communicate with any German, Nazi or anti-fascist,

including women and children. This was an unworkable
rule which was flouted openly but it created great bitterness, notably among non-Nazis. Brandt was also sceptical
about the results of the Potsdam Conference; to him the
settlement of the borders which involved a massive
movement of millions of people and a shift of the
German, Polish and Soviet borders to the west was
'unreasonably far reaching', although he did not consider
himself a nationalist.[1] Like many others Brandt was
haunted by visions of the Peace Treaty of Versailles after
World War I which had left Germany with a permanent
nationalist grudge which had helped Hitler come to
power.

Despite its drawbacks, Brandt found the International
Tribunal a worthwhile undertaking. At Nuremberg
members of the twenty two most important organizations
of the Third Reich were put on trial. These trials were
controversial: they were unpopular with the Germans as
'victors' justice'; there were no German judges and of
hundreds of accredited journalists only five were
Germans. The trials were also criticized abroad because
of their ambiguous legal basis; some of the legal categories were only created at Nuremberg and therefore
conflicted with a basic legal principle, *nulla poene sine
lege* i.e. a crime is only punishable if a law existed at the
time it was committed. However, for Brandt and gener-
ations of later historians they allowed a clear insight into
the details of the workings of the Third Reich. He was not
alone in being shocked by the personal mediocrity of the
perpetrators of unspeakable horrors – Hannah Arendt
later called it the 'banality of evil'. His reports to the
Scandinavian press were published in the spring of 1946 as
Criminals and Other Germans. The title was later distorted
by political enemies ('Germans and Other Criminals') in
an attempt to discredit his commitment to Germany.

The breaks in the proceedings at Nuremberg were
used by Brandt to make contact with prominent

members of the SPD, and notably its leader in the western zones, Kurt Schumacher with whom Brandt, however, had little in common. The bachelor Schumacher had spent years in Nazi prisons and concentration camps, he had lost an arm in World War I and was to lose a leg as a consequence of his ordeal in Nazi jails. It was not surprising that the energetic Brandt found Kurt Schumacher a rather difficult person whose 'authoritarian attitude, the almost fanatical tenacity with which he clung to his decisions, his way of over-emphasising national points of view' he found difficult to take. Brandt now had also to decide his future career. He rejected a first offer by the SPD to become mayor in his home town of Lübeck; the town had obviously become too small for him. Brandt feared problems over his Norwegian background, with the more humble party functionaries and the exhausting minutiae of urban reconstruction in a time of all-round shortages, were also not attractive to him. Eventually he accepted an offer by the Norwegian government to be press attaché in Berlin. Brandt went to Berlin as a member of the Norwegian delegation which involved the wearing of Norwegian uniform – a fact which later political opponents tried hard to exploit.

With his decision to go to Berlin for the Norwegians Brandt had decided against coming back to Germany as a German, but he felt so defensive about this that he even sent a duplicated letter of explanation of his decision to his friends: he wanted to act 'not from a narrowly nationalistic point of view but from that ... of how the individual could best serve the European rebirth and thereby that of German democracy'.[2] On a more realistic level, it was simply neither advantageous nor honourable to be a German at that time. (Later critics forget the loathing abroad of everything German at the end of the war.) Moreover, Norway had formed him and it was painful for him to cut the link with the country which had become his home. 'Political work in Germany on the other hand means community with people with whom one has not much in common.'[3]

Brandt started his post as Norwegian press attaché on 17 January 1947; his contract ran for one year. This period was to be a transitional one during which he could make a definite decision. After some debate he managed to be sent with the rank of 'major' which gave him a higher monthly salary. He was joined shortly afterwards by Rut, a Norwegian whom he had met when she worked in the press department of the Norwegian Embassy in Stockholm. Unlike his first wife she was more in tune with him socially and politically, having worked her way up in a bakery and as a needlewoman. At the time she met Brandt she was married to a railway worker (who died in 1946 of a lung disease). She came to Berlin in April 1947 and worked as Brandt's secretary. They were married on 4 September 1948. Their first son Peter was born a month later on 4 October 1948, followed by Lars in 1951 and Mathias in 1961. Their marriage lasted for over thirty years.

The problem of his political future was however not solved by his position as press attaché. The post was disappointing; he felt isolated in Berlin as a foreigner whose contacts with the German population remained limited. Moreover, he became aware that a small nation carried very little weight in international affairs. An appeal by the Minister Presidents of the German states, the *Länder*, to all exiled Germans to return and to help in the reconstruction of their country (June 1947), reinforced Brandt's conflict of loyalties and in September/October of that year he decided definitely to return to Germany. When the SPD leadership offered him the post of the party's liaison officer in Berlin he accepted and at the beginning of February 1948 he started his new job; on 1 July he obtained his German nationality back, his days of exile were over. At the same time the SPD leadership renewed his membership card which showed uninterrupted membership of the SPD since 1930 in accordance with the SPD's policy decision to cover up the divisions in the Left of the past.

RISE IN THE BERLIN SPD (1948–57)

The SPD in Berlin had got off the ground earlier than in the western zones; as early as 10 June 1945 Order No. 2 of the Soviet Military Government (which controlled the city alone until the arrival of the western allies on 1 July) had licensed democratic, anti-fascist parties. However, although the full range of parties had been allowed to operate it soon emerged that the Communists were much less popular than the SPD, and in order to disguise the KPD's weakness the Soviets forced through the unification of the two parties into a new Socialist Unity Party (SED) in April 1946. This was fiercely but unsuccessfully resisted by the SPD in Berlin and in the western zones under Schumacher. Despite Soviet pressure the Berlin SPD achieved a dominant position in the city and also beyond Berlin in the east; because it continued its illegal work there, it also influenced the western SPD largely because of the part played by Ernst Reuter who became mayor of Berlin in 1947, and who was one of the outstanding personalities of the post-war party. Reuter became Brandt's next political mentor.

Reuter returned from exile in Turkey in November 1946 at the age of 57. He was able to offer the SPD and Berlin two disparate but equally useful qualities: he had been involved in the town administration of Berlin in the 1920s and had become mayor of Magdeburg in 1930, a post from which the Nazis removed him in 1933. He had thus ample experience in local government which was badly needed in the chaos of post-war Berlin. But he was also one of the few non-Communist Germans with first hand knowledge of the Soviet Union and of Communism.

31

He had been a prisoner of war in Russia during World War I and the Russian Revolution, and had even obtained Lenin's confidence. In 1921 he became General Secretary of the German KPD, a post from which he was removed speedily owing to his opposition to the Comintern's attempts to interfere directly in the running of the party. In 1922 he joined the SPD. His view of Soviet policy never wavered, the Soviet Union was inspired by power politics only, with carefully calculated and planned moves. Only vigilance and strength would prevent the rest of Europe from falling under Soviet control in the way many east European countries had just experienced. Reuter therefore favoured strong defence, western integration, the speedy setting up of a West German state which was to establish close links with Berlin and a close cooperation with the other democratic parties; only a broad democratic front of all parties would make Berlin into the bastion of democratic freedom for which the United States would provide the vital support. On all these points Reuter (and later Brandt) came into fundamental conflict with Schumacher and the West German SPD who favoured a more independent course in the hope of speedy reunification. In Berlin Schumacher's line was supported by Franz Neumann, whereas Brandt whose official function as party linkman should have dictated such a line, in fact supported Reuter.

Brandt took over his post in Berlin within a few weeks of Reuter's election to mayor, although officially his appointment was finalised only in January 1948. There had been a last minute hitch when Schumacher showed doubts as to Brandt's suitability for the post; in view of their different personalities and backgrounds this was perhaps less surprising than that Brandt should have been considered for the post in the first place. The political scene could hardly have been more dramatic. In February 1948 the Communist coup against the democratically elected pro-Soviet government in Czechoslovakia became a key experience for Reuter and Brandt, which explained much of their later uncompromisingly anti-Communist stance. To secure Berlin's link with the west, Brandt in his reports recommended the moving of as many West German committees and other bodies as possible to Berlin; he conveyed the Berlin party's 'very vivid criticism' of Schumacher's decision not to take part in an all-party protest in Berlin on 18 March 1948.[4] Meanwhile the four power Control Council had ceased to function and the western Allies made proposals for the creation of a West German state. On 21 June 1948 a currency reform was carried through in the western zones and the Soviets imposed the blockade of Berlin in an attempt to prevent the imminent setting up of the FRG. The blockade was to last from 24 June 1948 to 12 May 1949. During this time the city was cut off from all land links with the west and survived only owing to the tremendous achievements of the American and British airforce which flew in supplies of all kinds in what became the 'Berlin Airlift'. Despite this allied commitment to the city, Berlin's position remained extremely vulnerable and Reuter (often accompanied by Brandt) travelled to the western zones of Germany, to London, Paris and even New York in order to canvass support for the city. He intervened openly in the negotiations between the Allies and the West German leaders and pressed for the acceptance of the Allied proposals; this gained him Schumacher's criticism that he was being 'more American than the Americans'. Reuter however had the strong support of the Berlin population (in elections in December 1948 the SPD polled a staggering 64.5 per cent) and that of the majority of the Berlin SPD. In the hour of the city's greatest need he had become its most eloquent and successful champion.

During the blockade Brandt became a public figure in the city. He had of course years of experience of confrontation with Communists and he now emerged as a skilled anti-Communist agitator with slogans such as 'Who relies on a Communist united front will die of it' or 'Berlin belongs to Europe and not to Siberia'. He recalls with admiration the courage with which the population of Berlin stood up to the hardships of the Blockade, which reminded him of the admirable resistance which the Norwegians had put up against the Nazi invaders.

Brandt's identification with Reuter brought him increasingly into conflict with Schumacher's line. His position as the SPD's link man in Berlin became untenable and Brandt gave it up at the end of 1949. He faced another career choice: Reuter offered him a post in the Berlin Town Administration (with responsibility for traffic – a post which Reuter himself had held in younger years). However, as in Lübeck after the war, Brandt decided against a job which involved a great deal of routine and opted instead for Bonn which had become the capital of the new Federal Republic where political decisions were now made. He was one of eleven Berlin representatives in the *Bundestag*. Although, once in Bonn, he busily worked for the interests of his city (he still attempted to get as many Bonn Ministries as possible to move to Berlin), his main sphere of interest remained the great political issues of the time. By 1952 he had become rapporteur of the Foreign Policy Committee, and gained recognition for his balanced accounts of its deliberations of the vital international treaties of the early 1950s. From now on he divided his time between Berlin and Bonn.

In Berlin the SPD fought out some fundamental battles which also influenced the course of the main SPD in West Germany. The end of the blockade left a terrible legacy of economic stagnation in the city which Reuter was successful in softening, by gaining for the city 10 per cent of all Marshall Aid going to Germany. Despite these obvious successes Reuter's policies did not find the undivided support of the Berlin (or the Bonn) SPD because Reuter and Brandt were looking for a modern people's party which could appeal to non-working class voters, whereas Neumann saw the SPD as the old working class organization of the days of the Weimar Republic. Neumann also felt that as party leader he should have more influence over policy whereas Reuter and Brandt refused to accept a 'tied mandate'. Moreover, Schumacher and Neumann disliked the coalition with the conservative CDU in Berlin, which Reuter and Brandt saw as indispensable in order to guarantee continued support from the (CDU) government in Bonn. Neumann wished to commit the Berlin SPD to the course followed by Schumacher in Bonn, that of relentless opposition. Close links with Bonn represented a further field of conflict. Reuter had accepted that Berlin should become a part of the West German legal and social system, this was far less progressive than that of Berlin. But for Reuter (and Brandt) foreign policy considerations predominated and this meant complete allegiance to the west.

Over the next few years these divisions intensified. Reuter was forced to implement lenient federal laws concerning the redeployment of National Socialist civil servants in Berlin. Moreover, the questions of the FRG's western integration and remilitarization in the wake of the Korean War became further issues on which the party disagreed. The 'Berliners' were behind the CDU which supported both in order to gain back for West Germany some international recognition and maintain its safety; but the bulk of the party was fearful that western integration would deepen Germany's division and was committed against remilitarization. The debates in Berlin were so heated that they culminated in an unsuccessful attempt by the SPD faction in Berlin's parliament to overthrow Reuter. However, subsequent SPD Congresses showed that the Berlin line was supported by the mayors of other important cities such as Brauer of Hamburg and Kaisen of Bremen. The disputes continued until, with the acceptance of the Godesberg Programme in 1959, the mayors had won the support of the main party.

Brandt supported the Reuter line but was more circumspect in the presentation of his views. This was illustrated well by his performance at the first SPD Congress after Schumacher's death in September 1952. With the fragile stability of the Berlin SPD in mind, but also in order not to expose himself too much in the SPD (West), Brandt refused to reject German remilitarization out of hand and criticized the party's perfectionism when it came to drawing up the institutions of European integration. He reminded the audience that the party had accepted Marshall Aid which in many ways had also not been exactly what the party had wanted. What was needed was flexibility and the readiness to cooperate in a new departure. One year later he was bolder, the Kremlin (and the German electorate) had to be clear about the fact that a Federal government led by Social Democrats would not conduct a spineless policy, but a policy of bringing together all states of the western world.

On 29 September 1953 Reuter suddenly died. Brandt gave the funeral oration, it was his first public appearance in front of the masses of the Berlin population. With Reuter dead and after the disastrous defeat of the SPD in the 1953 federal elections, the Berlin coalition government broke up. The post of mayor went to a member of the CDU. Reuter's death made Brandt the official heir of the former's policies in Berlin, but success in his continuing struggle with Neumann for the SPD leadership in Berlin had to wait several more years. The defeats at several elections affected Brandt more than they should have done, considering his comparatively new involvement in the Berlin party. However, he was a young man in a hurry.

His time in the West German SPD had also not yet come. At the SPD's annual congress in Berlin in July 1954 he stood for the party's national executive but obtained only 155 votes (as against Neumann with 270). The main reason for Brandt's defeat must be seen in his controversial views on defence which still came up against the solid rejection of any remilitarization by the party. Brandt could only restate his views and deplore the fact that in the past the German Left had, to its detriment, neglected the relationship of military power to democratic order.

However, the population of Berlin wholeheartedly endorsed his stance on defence. In elections in December 1954 the SPD there regained its absolute majority. The Social Democrat Otto Suhr became mayor and Brandt was elected President of the House of Representatives where he introduced a special ritual for the opening of sessions 'that this house pledges untiring efforts for the reunification of Germany' (after the construction of the Wall this was widened to 'and the removal of the Wall'). The post was largely representative but brought with it a large office and unlimited access to the press, which Brandt, with his intimate knowledge of its workings, used to excellent effect. He frequently called journalists in for briefing meetings at which coffee and brandy were served. He thus gradually built up invaluable support in the Berlin media. When Otto Suhr fell ill shortly after becoming mayor, Brandt automatically took on many of his representative duties; more and more he became the spokesman for Berlin. His picture and those of his family appeared frequently in the press; unlike the main SPD which rejected this manipulation of public opinion and earnestly tried to convince with the strength of their arguments, Brandt recognized the value of publicity.

But his main activity at this time was in the *Bundestag* where important decisions had to be made such as Germany's membership of NATO. He was convinced that Stalin's 'notes' of 1952 in which he offered German reunification on the basis of neutrality was a manoeuvre by the Soviets to prevent the FRG from joining the western defence organization (EDC); but unlike Adenauer and the western Allies he advocated that these proposals should at least be probed as to the seriousness of their intentions. On the other hand, Brandt remained unaware of the implications of the East Berlin rising in 1953; there had been an intense power struggle in the Kremlin after Stalin's death in March of that year with one of the factions apparently prepared to give up East Germany. The rising in Berlin strengthened the position of Walter Ulbricht who was now seen as indispensable by those who wished to hold on to the GDR.

Soviet policies ultimately provided Brandt with his breakthrough in Berlin when Soviet tanks crushed the uprising in Hungary in November 1956. The population of Berlin reacted particularly emotionally to these events. When a mass meeting was organized to protest against them the indignant population threatened to march to the Brandenburg Gate and to attack East German soldiers. Neumann's speech was ineffectual; at the last minute Brandt managed to divert part of the crowd away from its destination and to disperse it after the singing of the traditional army hymn to fallen soldiers (*Ich hatt' einen Kameraden* ...). Later at the Brandenburg Gate the same stratagem helped: after the defiant singing of the third verse of the *Deutschlandlied* the crowd calmed down. Brandt's later comment, that at times of crisis it helped to remember that his compatriots were fond of singing, indicates also to what extent he was able to gauge, to respond to and to manipulate the emotions of the masses. This ability was one of the reasons for his later political success when in the late 1960s he was able to articulate the desire for changed political values of a new post-war generation.

However, his immediate response to the Soviet clampdown was puzzling; at the Berlin party congress in January 1957 he called on the federal government in Bonn to use its modest possibilities to cooperate with the east. These ideas which foreshadowed the later *Ostpolitik* were however out of tune with Brandt's other utterances. The ambiguity of his political ideas at this period may be explained by his renewed attempt to be elected to the main SPD's executive committee. However, despite his cautious speech at the annual congress in Munich in July 1956 he failed again. While colleagues had a good time during a subsequent boating excursion, Brandt was seen sitting apart and with tears running down his cheeks. The disappointment was acutely felt.

On the other hand his rise to power in Berlin could no longer be stopped. In August 1957 Suhr died and on 3 October, Brandt was elected his successor. Only three months later, on 12 January 1958, he also became party leader in Berlin. The reason for his success was that, unlike Reuter, Brandt had in the meantime paid a great deal of attention to gaining more support at the lowest level of the party. He had set out systematically to gain control of the different districts, visiting local pubs and meeting as many of the party faithful as possible. He had also managed to assemble a group of young and enthusiastic followers around him, and it is a measure of the way in which Brandt was able to instil emotional personal loyalty, that two of them gave up their university studies to serve him. They admitted that as members of the war generation they were fascinated by Brandt's personality. One of them, Klaus Schütz, who later became Brandt's campaign manager, built up a card index with personal and political details of individual party members, so as to target Brandt's approach more precisely. With the concentration of the two offices in his hands his position was more powerful than that of Reuter who had never controlled the party machine. Despite this victory however, Brandt continued the fight against the Neumann wing, even expelling some prominent supporters of the latter from the party. Neumann himself ceased to play any role in Berlin but sat in the *Bundestag* as an innocuous backbencher from 1960 to 1969. The ruthlessness of Brandt's vendetta undoubtedly reflected the bitterness of the past struggle and the special *Frontstadt* (frontier town) mentality, where political issues as they had evolved between the two wings appeared as matters of life and death rather than mere differences of opinion. For Brandt personally it had been a hard fight (some observers believe it was the only open fight of Brandt's career) over eight years, and the emotions generated, left no room for compromise or conciliation.

CHANCELLOR CANDIDATE 1961 AND 1965

The positions of mayor of Berlin and leader of the Berlin party organization gave Brandt an excellent starting point for his advancement in the West German SPD. His first priority from now on was to play down the differences between the main SPD and the party in Berlin. Over the next few years he refined his already well-developed skill of 'double speak', the reconciling of opposite positions, or, as he put it himself, the art of the *sowohl-als-auch* (on the one hand – but on the other). This is well illustrated by his tactics on the question of nuclear arms, where Brandt basically supported the US position out of security considerations for Berlin, while the party embraced the popular rejection of nuclear arms. Brandt was able to convey the impression that he also rejected these weapons while at the same time continuing his pro-American line.

His way into the main SPD leadership was helped by circumstances which raised him to an international figure. In November 1958 Khrushchev revived the Berlin crisis by issuing an ultimatum: the Soviets demanded the change of Berlin into a demilitarized free city and allowed six months for the negotiating of their proposal. In January 1959 they put forward a draft Peace Treaty for Germany which was to consist of the two equal German states in another attempt to raise the status of the GDR.

In order to mobilize international support for Berlin, the Bonn government mounted an international publicity campaign and Brandt travelled the world as Berlin's representative, meeting all the leading statesmen and politicians. In New York he was greeted enthusiastically with a ticker tape parade. From May to August 1959 the foreign secretaries of the four powers met in Geneva to discuss the problem of Germany and Berlin. The Americans were seen to make too many concessions to the Soviets (including a reduced integration of Berlin with the west), and Brandt was sent by the Bonn government to remind the Americans of their obligations. He succeeded and the concessions were withdrawn. Brandt's international fame was such that his friend the Austrian Chancellor Kreisky recollected: 'The magazines of the world took hold of him and of his pretty wife. To be photographed with him was honourable and profitable. At that time some of his friends began to worry whether publicity might not get mixed up with or taken for policy.'[5]

However, his growing prominence strengthened the hand of the modernizers in the SPD where a prolonged process of re-orientation both in internal and foreign affairs was taking place which led to the adoption of a new programme at the Godesberg congress in November 1959. After the disastrous electoral defeats of 1953 and 1957 the party drew painful conclusions in lengthy debates. Again the Berlin influence can be traced in that the SPD narrowed its distance from the CDU by accepting the principles of the market economy (in stark contrast to its previous advocacy of socialism) and of national defence (against all shades of anti-militarism hitherto prevalent in the party's official pronouncements). The SPD thus began to turn from a traditional workers' party into a wider 'People's Party'; for the first time the party admitted openly, that in so doing it was led by considerations of power politics. In order to win at the polls the

SPD had to present an attractive programme, even if this meant coming close to that of the political enemy. Brandt's position on the programme was in-keeping with his overall approach to politics. He would have preferred not to have a detailed programme at all, but a short and flexible action programme instead. During the debate he spoke only once and then, perhaps characteristically, to underline its publicity value: '[The programme] is essentially ... a modern statement which will make it more difficult for our enemies to fight the reality rather than a travesty of German Social Democracy'. The change in the party's foreign policy stance was announced by Herbert Wehner, a leading party member, in an important speech to the *Bundestag* in June 1960 in which he demanded a 'common foreign policy' with the CDU in view of the Soviet threat to Berlin; the West German SPD had endorsed the line of the Berlin branch.

The modernization of the SPD's image had become necessary if the party was to have a chance of avoiding another defeat at the next election in September 1961. It also needed a more attractive candidate for Chancellor than Schumacher's worthy successor, Ollenhauer. Brandt with his international renown, his youth and image of modernity seemed the best alternative and on 24 August 1960 he became the party's official candidate. His choice was mainly due to the growing weight of younger party members (the *Frontgeneration*) but there was still considerable opposition to Brandt and the new party line which emerged in Hanover in November 1960. Rather than endorsing the candidate, a sizeable minority on the left opposed him and insisted again on a debate on nuclear arms, when it had been intended to demonstrate party unity at this pre-election meeting and to instil optimism in the members. Brandt was re-elected to the central committee with a reduced majority. It was not only a matter of politics which weakened Brandt's standing. By now his Berlin clique was becoming more prominent in the main SPD and they were frequently disliked for their youth and political cynicism. Brandt was also showing too much independence from the party when in his official speech of acceptance of the candidature he stated: 'I am the candidate of this party for an office whose occupant determines the guidelines of policy and who is responsible to the whole of parliament and thereby to [the whole of] the people. It is perhaps not popular when I declare here that I cannot simply be the executor of the party's [wishes].' The SPD tactics were to fight an American style personalized campaign where issues were played down and the candidate personally canvassed the electorate, touring the country in a special train and meeting as many voters as possible face to face. The youthful Brandt was presented as the German Kennedy, this reached even into his private life with his wife's pregnancy during the campaign (like Jackie Kennedy the previous year). This approach seemed all the more plausible as Brandt's counterpart, Konrad Adenauer, was by now an old man of eighty-five who the previous year had himself toyed with the idea of retirement from the office of Chancellor to that of the representative President of the Republic. However, Adenauer had decided to stay on as Chancellor and although he lost a great deal of public sympathy, his position was not as weak as the SPD had assumed. There was the *Kanzlerfaktor*, the prestige of office which always worked in favour of the incumbent. Adenauer could also point to the continuing growth in prosperity, and to his record in providing safety and stability for West Germany. There were other residual factors which were still operating against the SPD. The party could still be labelled socialist and thus somehow equated with what went on behind the iron curtain; it had been in total opposition to everything Adenauer had achieved and its conversion at Godesberg was of too recent a date and had come too suddenly to be entirely convincing.

The SPD's main strategy was therefore to bank on the apparently favourable comparison between Brandt and Adenauer, but this had a boomerang effect on the SPD. It soon emerged that Brandt's past and especially his emigration from Nazi Germany provided opponents and notably the CDU/CSU with an easy target for their propaganda.[6] The leader of the Bavarian CSU, Franz Josef Strauss set the tone in a speech in February 1961: 'We may be allowed to ask Herr Brandt one question: what were you doing during the twelve years outside [Germany]? We know what we were doing inside ...' Another prominent member of the CDU who later rose to Minister of Defence, Kai-Uwe von Hassel, stated 'I do not deny my nationality (*Volks-und Staatsangehörigkeit*) because of personal or other advantages, I cannot leave this community of destiny (*Schicksalsgemeinschaft*) when it appears personally dangerous to me, and join it again when the risk has passed'. The CDU recommended electoral speakers to let it be known that Brandt had been 'a traitor to the fatherland'. Christian politicians tried to gain political kudos out of his illegitimate birth and compared his change of name to that of Hitler whose real name had been Schickgrubler. Adenauer referred to Brandt: 'If one of my political opponents has been treated with the greatest consideration, it was Herr Brandt, alias Frahm ...' The CDU/CSU campaign was one of the dirtiest national election campaigns in the history of the western world. 'What is perhaps more surprising is the fact that these attacks against Brandt fell on such fertile ground. In the summer of 1960 about 40 per cent of West Germans believed that emigrés should not hold ministerial office'[7]; it seems that National Socialist propaganda which had depicted emigrés as irresponsible and untrustworthy was having long lasting effect. But the reason for this must also be seen in West Germany's political culture of the time. The fast onset of the Cold War had prevented a more fundamental reckoning with National

Socialism. Instead the reconstruction of the country, security, the development of a viable democratic system and the creation of prosperity had brought about a political consensus which was based on the tacit exclusion of the past, and which was shared by all major political forces, including the SPD. This consensus was put in jeopardy by emigrés. They represented the 'other Germany'; they were a living reminder that there had been an alternative to National Socialism. They were thus threatening the consensus and they had to be fought with all means. This explains the extraordinary ferocity of the campaign against a man like Brandt. On the other hand Brandt's and the SPD's lack of adequate response is equally revealing. They were part of the consensus and therefore tried to play down their own political past (however honourable it might have been in anti-fascist terms). Brandt simply rejected the reality of the problem when he declared at the party congress in Hanover in November 1960: 'I have little need for a justification of the fact that already in my youth I was a consistent opponent [of National Socialism]'. He never mentioned his exile in public; his writings during the years in exile were not available in German translation. Speculation and innuendo thus had ample ground in which to flourish, and although Brandt took the worst perpetrators to court and won every time, something always stuck in the public mind. Moreover, he showed his own sensitivity to these attacks too openly not to create the impression that he might have something to hide.

Brandt did not openly counterattack but tried to lift the campaign to a different level. Instead of the vilification which he received, Brandt advocated realism (*Sachlichkeit*) in politics. In this way all problems of the country could be solved. This necessarily led to generalizing and unconvincing platitudes.

But Brandt's cause was given substantial last minute help by a new Berlin crisis, the construction of the Berlin Wall between 13 and 16 August which sealed off the two parts of the city completely from each other. This was the only means by which the East Germans were able to stop the incessant outflow of their most able and mobile people to the west (as many as 30,415 in July 1961 alone). Brandt had anticipated a new crisis particularly after Khrushchev had uttered new threats against the city at the beginning of 1961. In March Brandt had travelled to the USA to prime the new American President John F. Kennedy about the background to Khrushchev's demands prior to their planned summit meeting in Vienna in June 1961. Brandt's fears that the USA were too ready to make concessions seemed justified when at Vienna Khrushchev announced a separate peace treaty with the GDR and Kennedy only referred to the rights of *West* Berlin, thus abandoning any claim to influence in the whole city under the four power agreement. This shift in American policy was expressed openly on 25 July in Kennedy's three 'essentials' of the US position in Berlin: the right of presence for the western powers, the right to free access through East Germany and the safeguarding of the political freedom and viability of West Berlin. The American troops were reinforced but there was no denying the fact that the western powers signalled the limitations of their claims to West Berlin alone. The construction of the Wall therefore elicited only a mild verbal rebuke of the Soviet Union from the western powers and that after a delay of several days. Adenauer behaved in a similarly remote fashion, refusing even to visit the city and continuing his election tour. He even claimed that this new Berlin crisis had been orchestrated by the Soviets to help their German friends, the SPD. The SPD on the other hand did use the crisis to best effect. Brandt gained enormous publicity. In the first days immediately after the Wall was built he appeared for ten hours on West German TV screens as against Adenauer's two. The party had new posters printed: 'Germans! Think of Berlin!' The papers published advertisements: 'Now everyone knows. Willy Brandt is a man of decisiveness and peace. Berlin is the example for Germany'.

The response in Berlin and in West Germany was a totally different, emotional outburst. There was fear of a new war because a firm response by the western powers was expected, particularly from the USA. The disappointment at the latter's inaction was particularly bitter. *Bild*, the daily mass circulation tabloid, led with a banner headline: 'The West does NOTHING!' This indignation spread to Adenauer's failure to visit the city. On 16 August a mass protest meeting took place in front of the Town Hall at which Brandt (who had hurried back to Berlin from canvassing in West Germany on 13 August) faced a task not dissimilar to that during the Hungarian uprising, to give vent to the audience's emotions while containing them and directing them away from potentially disastrous aggression against East German soldiers or policemen. He succeeded in masterly fashion and his popularity with the Berliners undoubtedly rested on his ability to give expression to their frustrations. But he also guided the Berliners to the acceptance of the inevitable when shortly afterwards he stated 'We must learn to live with the Wall. We must think – patiently and thoroughly – how we can make it transparent. It will not be removed but it must be made superfluous in a wider context'. Here was Brandt's later *Ostpolitik* in a nutshell.

The election results were a disappointment for the SPD and its candidate and bore out the success of a right wing campaign. Despite the severe blow which the construction of the Berlin Wall represented for the CDU/CSU and Adenauer, the SPD could only muster respectable gains of 4.4 per cent and had increased its share of the vote to 36.2 per cent. The CDU's vote held, albeit much reduced to 45.4 per cent, a sharp drop from its previous absolute majority of 50.2 per cent. But in view of the obvious failure of Adenauer's foreign policy this drop was not as substantial as might have been expected. Adenauer still commanded enormous respect as the man who had brought back prosperity and a measure of respectability. The SPD could not match this and would not have done better with a less vulnerable (Chancellor) candidate; on the contrary, it was due to Brandt's great success in Berlin that the SPD was able to increase its vote in the way it did.

The defeat did not deter the SPD from continuing its course of unity with the CDU, a line which was pushed notably by Wehner who was convinced that in order to be fully acceptable to the German electorate the SPD had to emerge from its role of opposition party into demonstrating its ability to govern, if need be even by going into a coalition with the CDU. Even a coalition under Adenauer was contemplated. Brandt favoured either an all-party coalition or cooperation with the Free Democrats (FDP). However, the time for such arrangements had not yet come. In December 1961 Brandt withdrew from Bonn, resigning his *Bundestag* mandate and letting it be known that he would not be automatically available as candidate for Chancellor again at the next election in 1965. He returned to Berlin as he had promised the Berliners he would do if not elected Federal Chancellor.

The Wall had a disastrous economic effect on the city but even worse was perhaps the human aspect which was brought home to the population in an incident on 17 August 1962 when two eighteen-year-old East Berlin workers tried to escape to the west by scaling the wall. One of them, Peter Fechner, was shot by the East German guards, fell back on the eastern side of the Wall and was left to bleed to death by the East Germans. His cries for help could be heard in the west where people were unable to intervene. Public indignation in West Berlin again ran high. Again Brandt was called upon to restrain the masses from acting provocatively.

The Fechner incident illustrated yet again the powerlessness of the West when confronting determination and readiness to use force by the East. It must have been a contributory factor towards a lengthy period of depression which Brandt suffered in the autumn of 1962 and which expressed itself in periods of withdrawal, excessive alcohol consumption and sexual affairs. However, in February 1963 the Berlin electorate clearly acknowledged his services to the city with a thumping majority for the SPD of 61.9 per cent. Brandt's fortunes were clearly rising again. He began a period of political reorientation. In Berlin this led to the end of the long established coalition with the CDU (which had pressured Brandt into abandoning contacts with the Soviets in order to try and improve the situation in Berlin), and the beginning of a cooperation with the liberal FDP. In foreign policy his thinking changed direction and came more into line with that outside Germany and notably with that of the USA. The successful resolution of the Cuban missile crisis of October 1962 had led to the beginning of a phase of coexistence between the superpowers. Brandt visited Kennedy on several occasions and in June 1963 Kennedy visited Berlin (the occasion of his famous *Ich bin ein Berliner* speech). Kennedy's views, expressed in greater detail in an address to the students of Berlin's Free University, that a future solution of the Berlin problem had to start by accepting the realities of the situation and to work from there, found an echo in a speech which Brandt's close colleague Egon Bahr made in July. For the first time it was advocated that change in Germany had to come through a process of getting closer to the eastern bloc (*Wandel durch Annäherung*). This was of course the core of what later became Brandt's *Ostpolitik*. One immediate result was the negotiation with East Berlin of an agreement which enabled West Berliners to visit their East Berlin relatives for Christmas for the first time since August 1961.

The excellent election results in February 1963 and

Brandt's return to the public's attention as a result of the publicity gained during Kennedy's visit, also led to his enhanced standing in the SPD. Brandt's influence there had been diminishing because although he had been made Deputy Chairman in 1962 he had been largely absent from Bonn. Moreover, without a seat in the *Bundestag* he was without a platform from which to make his weight in the party felt. When in the autumn of 1963 the leadership question of the SPD became an open problem with Ollenhauer's health visibly failing, it was Herbert Wehner, in charge of party organization and by now *eminence grise* behind the scenes who determined that Brandt should become Ollenhauer's successor. This decision was endorsed by a special party congress in February 1964 when Brandt was also chosen to be again the party's candidate for Chancellor at the next election. Despite these important functions however, Brandt was only partially in control; his powerful deputies Wehner and Erler were in charge of party organization and the party in the *Bundestag* respectively. Wehner later claimed that Brandt had been a mere *Gallionsfigur* (figure head), an obvious exaggeration, although Brandt's main asset lay less in the party establishment than in his attraction for the mass of the party members and the voters. On the contrary, in the long run it worked to Brandt's advantage that he was not closely involved in the party's more controversial policies during these years, such as the cooperation between government and SPD over the Emergency Laws (which gave the government wide powers to suspend civil liberties). On the other hand he also worked for the SPD's unity approach with the CDU when in 1963 Adenauer was made an Honorary Citizen of Berlin on the occasion of his resignation. But the occasion went beyond narrow party confines with Brandt stressing the historic dimension of the moment. 'With honour goes honesty. We do not want to pretend here that there has been no tension between Adenauer and

Reuter and no conflict between Adenauer and Brandt. But none of this changes the fact that the German capital honours the man who for fourteen years stood at the head of the free Germany and that even the political opponent pays this man respect.' It was this sort of gesture which explains his later great success with German youth.

In the short run his lack of influence was frustrating Brandt's intentions. He did not succeed in getting his Berlin confidant Bahr accepted as party speaker which would have given him some control over the projection of his image. (There was still resentment in the party against the great influence of the Berlin 'mafia' in 1961). He also had less influence over the 1965 election campaign than in 1961. The party election managers decided to play down the role of the candidate and to stress the SPD government team instead. This reflected the fact that in 1965 Brandt was not as attractive a candidate as he had been previously, although Brandt himself did not accept this. By 1965 the 'Berlin factor' had lost much of its appeal. Moreover, whereas in 1961 he faced the ageing Adenauer and could radiate modernity which could speak to the whole people, the political landscape had changed in the meantime. Adenauer had resigned in October 1963 and had been replaced by Ludwig Erhard, the 'father' of the economic miracle. Erhard had only recently joined the CDU and had always steered clear of political infighting. It was thus easy to present him as the true 'People's Chancellor', a label which Brandt had been trying to claim for himself. Moreover, the old attacks against Brandt's past were repeated and even Erhard took part in them: he had already worked on plans for the German currency reform when Brandt 'had not even become a German citizen again'.[8] The whisper campaign against Brandt over several years had also had its effect. Brandt had lost much support in the German press; in particular Axel

51

Springer's influential *Bild Zeitung* had turned against him since Brandt, with ideas such as *Wandel durch Annäherung*, was seemingly abandoning Germany's national interests.

In the face of these attacks Brandt and the SPD strove for *Gemeinsamkeiten* (unity) of all German parties. But this 'sweet reasonableness' came across as boring; the main SPD slogan 'Safe is Safe – therefore SPD' in the words of a political opponent was 'the absolute nothing'.[9] In November 1964, 71 per cent of all Germans wanted Erhard as Chancellor and only 26 per cent Brandt. When compared with the voting intentions for a party (37 per cent for the SPD, 30 per cent for the CDU)[10] it became clear that Brandt was no longer an electoral asset.

Despite these statistics the SPD and Brandt expected victory, or at least such a close result that the SPD would be involved in the next government. (The party had achieved excellent results in recent regional elections.) The results came therefore as a great disappointment. Erhard had achieved the second best vote for the CDU/CSU in the history of the Federal Republic with 47.6 per cent. But although the SPD achieved its best result so far, with 39.3 per cent the party was still far from its target. For Brandt this was a bitter blow. He was deeply hurt by what he called the *Dreckkampagne* (dirty campaign) against his past and showed it in a first TV interview: 'I came back to Germany with clean hands, with clean hands ... I have not come through this campaign unscathed ...' He announced that he would not be the party's candidate again in 1969. But he did not resign as party leader which meant that he remained in the running when the general political scene changed dramatically one year later.

For the time being he returned to Berlin and again was overcome by depression, which was all the worse this time because his personal contribution to the campaign had been ambivalent. It was painful to have to realize that he might have been a hindrance rather than a help to his party. At the age of fifty two he felt that both privately and politically 'real life' was now behind him. 'The year 1965 was for me a caesura, a break – and that was beneficial. Since then the decisions which I had to make were easier, because – even measured against what others expected of me – they no longer had to do with what one can become but rather with what one wants to do'.[11] This to some extent referred to the way in which he had allowed others to dictate his image during the two previous election campaigns. The fiction of 'young Kennedy' had misled him into believing that the public could be manipulated into any direction and that, given the right technique, anything could be done in politics. In the course of this self-analysis he began to work systematically through his time in exile and later in the year a book (*Draussen*) with extracts of his writings in German during that period was published. He settled back into the Berlin routine but developments in Bonn were soon to change his fortunes dramatically.

The Grand Coalition, 1966–9 $\mathbf{3}$

THE FORMATION OF THE GRAND COALITION

The fortunes of Chancellor Erhard, relatively inexperienced in politics, and under constant criticism from former Chancellor Adenauer, deteriorated rapidly after his election victory. He came to grief in the area of his greatest former success, the economy. In 1966 it went into a minor recession with 4.5 per cent inflation and 100,000 unemployed against 600,000 job vacancies and 1.4 million guest workers in the country. However, the media and experts predicted an almost inevitable worsening of the 'crisis' and this irrational anxiety was also widespread in the public at large; 20 per cent of those questioned in a survey in 1966 thought that a major crisis as in 1929 was certain and a further 40 per cent thought it highly likely. Only 13 per cent thought it was unlikely and only 3 per cent were certain it would not come at all.[1] To many the parallel with Germany in the early 1930s could also be seen in the temporary increase in votes for the right wing neo-Nazi party, the NPD.

After a humiliating trip to the USA whose government refused to scale down demands for a higher German contribution to the costs of US troops in Germany, Erhard was unable to present a balanced budget for 1967 and was forced from office on 1 October 1966 by the resignation of the FDP ministers in his coalition. His party, the CDU, in the meantime had found not only a new candidate for Chancellor, Kurt Georg Kiesinger, the Prime Minister of Baden-Württemberg, but also a new coalition partner, the SPD.

A coalition between the biggest two parties was a new departure in West German politics and signalled the end of the FRG's formative period. However, for all concerned there were risks involved in the venture. For the CDU it meant giving the SPD the respectability of government office and thus enhancing its enemy's standing; for the SPD, involvement with the CDU would bring about tension with the party's rank and file and for the FDP the danger that as the only opposition party it might be squashed between the giants; indeed the CDU at this time planned a change of the electoral law from proportional representation to majority voting which would have excluded the FDP from a future role in Bonn. (The SPD whose consent was needed to this change of the constitution finally killed the project when it voted against it at its annual party congress in Nuremberg in 1968.)

For the SPD a coalition with the CDU under Kiesinger was all the more difficult as the latter had been a member of the NSDAP, and this was one of the reasons why Brandt preferred a coalition with the FDP. The liberals were however divided on most policy issues, which would have made a highly unstable basis for government. Most other leading Social Democrats such as Wehner and Helmut Schmidt therefore favoured a coalition with the CDU. The advantage of being able to display the party's expertise and commitment in government for the first time in the Federal Republic's history, outweighed for them the political affiliations past and present of some of their coalition partners. Wehner and Schmidt therefore carried out much of the negotiations and presented Brandt, delayed in Berlin by fog for the crucial meeting, with *faits accomplis* which Brandt reluctantly accepted.

Brandt played a comparatively minor role in these events for another reason also. On 28 October he suffered an attack of coughing and suffocation. He was found unconscious, blue in the face, and he was rushed to hospital. He believed that he was dying. Although the medical diagnosis of what happened was unclear and he recovered quickly Brandt seemed more reticent in taking an active role than might otherwise have been the case. However, once the decision was taken, he made an important contribution to persuading the parliamentary faction of the SPD, which feared a 'sell out' of the party's principles, to approve the coalition. But he was unwilling to become a minister himself; he wished to remain outside the cabinet and concentrate on the party leadership. If he had to represent the SPD inside it he considered a small ministry such as research or health best suited to his purposes of demonstrating the SPD's will to introduce reforms in Germany. Eventually Brandt was persuaded by Wehner to go for what was his due as party leader and what would bring the SPD most kudos, the post of Vice-Chancellor and Foreign Secretary.

The Grand Coalition was billed as the 'cabinet of reconciliation' because in it there came together for the first time the representatives of Nazi and anti-fascist Germany, of the present right (Franz Josef Strauss and von Hassel) and left (Wehner – an ex-Communist – and Schmidt). However, for Brandt it has been called a 'cabinet of impositions' (*Zumutungen*). He now had to cooperate with Strauss and von Hassel who only a very short time ago had vilified him because of his past. Moreover, Kiesinger, had wanted to become Foreign Secretary himself and although amiable in public, treated Brandt not as an equal but with condescension. Cabinet sessions were filled with interminable fruitless debates at which Brandt often kept a frustrated silence. However, there was good cooperation between Kiesinger and Wehner, and the other Social Democrats and their conservative counterparts. Brandt's unease on the other hand, a mixture of political principle and personal hurt, remained only thinly veiled in the cooperation with Kiesinger over the beginnings of a new German foreign policy.

THE FOREIGN SECRETARY

Brandt took to his new post immediately and obviously enjoyed it. Everything in his background had prepared him for the task: his ability to view German problems in an international setting gained through the years in exile and his role in Berlin; his awareness of historical processes, his fluency in several foreign languages and his personal charm. In particular, the very stance against National Socialism which had brought him so much vilification from critics at home now worked in his favour abroad where he was universally respected; he represented the 'better Germany'. Brandt could use his open acknowledgement of German responsibility for Nazi crimes to speak up for German and European interests with much greater credibility than his predecessors had been able to do.

He took over a ministry whose staff had been recruited by a succession of conservative ministers. However, Brandt limited the number of dismissals and even recalled a conservative expert out of retirement, although his close collaborators from the Berlin days, Bahr and Schütz, were also given important posts. With this moderation and his unstinting hard work Brandt soon won the recognition of his staff. Although he claimed that it took a year to master the ins and outs of international affairs he was in fact able to make an important policy speech at Geneva in September 1968.

During the last Adenauer years the Federal Republic had drifted into comparative international isolation. Its persistent demands for reunification had got out of step with the general tendency towards détente after the Cuba crisis and the objective of improved relations with the Soviet Union among her closest allies and within NATO. Under Erhard the Federal Republic began the process of reorientation of its foreign policy with a cautious 'policy of movement' towards the east and the establishment of trade missions with Romania and Yugoslavia; the process culminated in the Peace Note of March 1966 in which the German government pledged its readiness to work towards détente and demilitarization. It also renounced the use of force towards the east, although neither the GDR nor the Oder-Neisse line was mentioned. The Grand Coalition continued this phase of reappraisal of West Germany's position in Europe and the world. In June 1967 Chancellor Kiesinger outlined the aims of his government (incorporating many of Brandt's ideas). The German objective was a European Peace Order, a restructuring of Europe in the wake of a balancing of interests between the alliance systems in east and west. In this process the divided parts of Germany would grow together. However, the government's firm refusal to countenance the recognition of the GDR as a political reality put a stop to far reaching changes in the FRG's actual foreign policy. It was here that Brandt as Chancellor was to advance to a more flexible position.

Although he came to office without a detailed programme, a basic framework for his foreign policy existed. This was partly based on ideas put forward by Jean Monnet, one of the founders of the European integration movement and another of Brandt's 'fatherly friends'. Brandt was a member of his Action Committee for the United States of Europe, twice inviting it to hold sessions in Bonn even after he had become Chancellor. Monnet's ideas on European unity (repeated frequently and 'with the obstinacy of a preacher' according to Brandt), but particularly those calling for equality between Europe and the US and peaceful coexistence with the Soviet Union, were later acted on in Brandt's *Ostpolitik*. Within this broad framework the objective of Brandt's foreign policy at this stage seemed to be a European security system which should be precondition and part of the European Peace Order for which Brandt and his advisors saw two models; either the existing alliances could enter into a new relationship with each other, or NATO and the Warsaw Pact could be dismantled step by step and replaced by something new. Brandt favoured the first model, the evolutionary development out of existing structures. This European Peace Order was not only defined in security terms, it should make new forms of cooperation possible. For Brandt the basis of this new order should be self determination for all European nations, including the Germans. In addition Brandt believed that the rights of national minorities, human rights and freedom of information formed important elements of this new order which was moreover to develop in the direction of socialist values. Brandt saw the future of the European Community for example as a social union. However, these were long-term aims although as such they were the basis of the later *Ostpolitik*. For the time being the continued existence of NATO and West Germany's integration in it was indispensable. A first aim must be the achievement of détente without which there would be no chance of an improvement in the 'German Question'. Prior to coming to office he had approached this from a policy of strength, warning his colleagues in the SPD Council in December 1965, that a policy of détente in the coming years must under no circumstances be weakness; it could be destroyed if the US were defeated in Vietnam. At the same time he saw the necessity of direct contacts with the Soviet Union and in early 1966 he had several meetings with the Soviet Ambassador in East Berlin, Abrassimov, through the mediation of the Swedish consul in Berlin. Although these talks were secret they were well leaked and caused the Erhard government some embarrassment over Brandt's loyalty to the official foreign policy. For Brandt and the SPD however these independent initiatives were a means to develop their own foreign policy profile without open confrontation with the government. This was to remain the SPD's and Brandt's tactics during the Grand Coalition, where they stressed the common policy with the CDU but interpreted it in their own way. They thus succeeded in endorsing joint policies in the Cabinet and yet were the opposition in foreign policy at the same time. This was the purpose of numerous unofficial statements on *Ostpolitik* emanating from the Foreign Office (*Ostpolitisches Geriesel* as opponents would have it[2]) which Brandt never stopped. In this way the SPD developed the invaluable skill of combining in its policies towards the east in general, and the GDR in particular, new with old, tradition and movement, security and progress which was to give the party the edge in the elections of 1969.

At the SPD annual conference in Dortmund in June 1966 Brandt had given a comprehensive overview of his ideas on international affairs. For him the successful conduct of foreign affairs had to be based on a recognition of the 'mutuality of interests' of all concerned. The concept was simple, a satisfied self interest of all partners was the best guarantee for longterm stability. For Germany in the 1960s this meant recognizing the status quo which the reality of Germany's military defeat in World War II had created. This implied a recognition of the Oder-Neisse line as the border between a future German nation state and Poland and – although Brandt shied away from a recognition of the GDR as a foreign country – agreement that there should be 'a qualified, orderly and in terms of time limited next-to-each-other (*Nebeneinander*) of the two German territories.' Only if the Federal Republic worked alongside the process of détente initiated by the superpowers (instead of hindering it as had been the case in the later days of Adenauer, and to some extent still under Erhard), could German politics gain in influence and weight. The overall objective for Brandt was to win an independent role for Germany in east and west. 'We do not want – in the east or the west of our country – to become the extended workbench of superpowers ...' In his search for a role for Germany Brandt was an admirer of de Gaulle and his independent European stance for France. Like him he searched for a national self-awareness for Germany, which for the divided country he found in the concept of the 'one German nation' which continued despite political divisions. Above all, the Germans should find a new self confidence. 'We Germans must not forget our history. But we can also not continually utter confessions of guilt ... we must intensely, responsibly ask for our right to self determination, to national self realization and with this make our contribution to the healing [of the wounds] of Europe's centre'. This was a task which needed the cooperation of the entire international community but Brandt sought to increase Germany's freedom of manoeuvre by lessening her dependence on the superpowers. He castigated the latter's inactivity notably after Stalin's death and over the construction of the Berlin Wall; it had become increasingly clear that the interests of the big powers did not necessarily coincide with those of Germany.

When, after ten months as Foreign Secretary, Brandt addressed the students of Berlin University on 8 October 1967 in a ceremony commemorating the 100th anniversary of one of his predecessors during the Weimar Republic, Rathenau, many of these ideas re-appeared, and the concept of mutual interests was now specifically applied to the Soviet Union, whose hostility and suspicions towards Germany had so far been the stumbling block to all movement on the 'German question'. The logical culmination of this policy was the renunciation of the use of force. But Brandt was also intensely aware 'that the ice of [international] confidence [in Germany] is still thin'[3] and he was therefore prepared to make gestures to improve this confidence. It was here that he saw parallels between Rathenau's position and his own; the former had been murdered because he was seeking to improve Germany's lot by fulfilling the clauses of the Treaty of Versailles. Brandt was the victim of *Rufmord* (murder of his reputation) because to his enemies he seemed to be making too many, needless concessions (*Vorleistungen*) without immediate, tangible results.

These objections to his policies existed not only on the right where they might have been expected, but also in the SPD itself where sections of the party were still committed to the demands for German unity and the representation of refugee interests. It seemed that history was repeating itself, as in the 1950s it was the 'Berlin mafia' around Brandt with the concept of 'change through rapprochement' which was pushing the more conservative elements in the party in a new direction. On the other hand, Brandt initially found cautious support from Chancellor Kiesinger for a 'policy of humane improvements' towards the east European states.

In his first government statement Kiesinger, reflecting Brandt's ideas, declared his intention to free West Germany's foreign policy from the 'juristic fictions and bureaucratic obstacles' of the past and to seek contacts with officials of the GDR in the interests of the people living there. The GDR should no longer be isolated, but full legal recognition was to be avoided. The Hallstein Doctrine of the 1950s which had dominated West German foreign policy to the east was to be amended, whereas previously the West Germans would break off diplomatic relations with any state which recognized the GDR. This was now changed as far as the east Europeans were concerned, they were deemed not to have had a policy choice: their recognition of the GDR having been prescribed by Moscow. Likewise, the borders between Germany and Czechoslovakia as drawn up at the Munich Conference in 1938 were declared null and void.

A first and rapid success of these initiatives came in the form of diplomatic relations established between the Federal Republic and Romania in January 1967, but it soon transpired that further progress would be much more difficult. Negotiations for the establishment of diplomatic relations with Hungary and Czechoslovakia soon stalled. Far from being enthusiastic about Bonn's new overtures the Soviet, and in particular the East German government, saw in them an imperialist threat. The support of the world's Communist and Workers' Parties was enlisted (Karlsbad Conference, April 1967), and in a reversal of the Hallstein Doctrine, an Ulbricht Doctrine was promulgated whereby a member of the Warsaw Pact was able to establish diplomatic relations with the FRG only after the latter had recognized the GDR, the Oder-Neisse line and West-Berlin as an 'independent political entity'. In particular the GDR itself launched a policy of *Abgrenzung* (delimitation) against the FRG. Thus, on 20 February 1967 a Citizenship Law was promulgated which was based on the existence of two German states and thus removed the principle of one German nationality, which so far was still part of the GDR constitution. In April 1967 Kiesinger offered the GDR government sixteen proposals for the improvement of everyday life there, but in his reply GDR Prime Minister Stoph only reiterated old demands for normal relations between FRG and GDR. The exchange of letters which continued into September 1967 remained entirely fruitless and led to serious divisions in the coalition. Whereas the SPD and Brandt held that every contact with the GDR was useful, increasingly sharp criticism of the 'Recognition Party' emanated from the right wing of the CDU. This not only applied to the SPD but to the entire spectrum of public opinion in the FRG (such as the weeklies *Die Zeit* and *Der Spiegel*) which advocated a more open approach to the GDR.

Equally frustrating were the coalition's attempts to make progress with the east through formal declarations of the renunciation of the use of force against other powers. The Soviet Union not only insisted on such a declaration between the FRG and the GDR, which implied recognition of the latter, but invoked its right under the enemy state clause of Articles 53 and 107 of the UN Charter to intervene in the affairs of the FRG should the latter threaten international peace. It even published the correspondence containing the German offer in an attempt to cause the government and Brandt maximum embarrassment. Both the Soviet Union and GDR protested against the presence in West Berlin of members and groups of the West German government and in April 1968 the GDR banned members of the FRG government from transit through its territory. A climax was reached on 28 April when the Mayor of Berlin who happened to be President of the Upper House, the *Bundesrat* (a job which rotates between the heads of the states) was prevented from reaching the city by land. In June a formal passport and visa requirement for journeys between the two Germanies was introduced.

Brandt saw in these reactions the responses of profoundly insecure powers and advocated the continuation of the course of rapprochement with the east. At the SPD conference in Nuremberg in March 1968 he demanded that the government should treat the GDR in the same way as other East European states, i.e. extend the declaration against the use of force fully to East Germany; the government should also declare its intention to 'recognize the existing borders, in particular to respect and recognize Poland's border with the west'. In June at the meeting of NATO's Council of Ministers at Reikjavik he reiterated the renunciation of every attempt by the FRG 'to change by force the existing social structures in the other part of Germany'. However, the CDU was not prepared to support Kiesinger further in this direction, and the latter with an eye on the elections in the coming year grew more timid. The turning point came with the Soviet invasion of Czechoslovakia on 20 August 1968 which ended an experiment there to create a system of 'Socialism with a Human Face'. The promulgation of the Brezhnev Doctrine in November by which the USSR reserved for itself the right to intervene in any country within its sphere of influence, demonstrated the iron grip it had over the entire area and its determination to enforce it ruthlessly.

It seemed to a majority in the CDU that Moscow had interpreted the German government's overtures as weakness; they advocated a return to the uncompromising principles of Adenauer. The SPD on the other hand argued that Moscow had been placed on the defensive by Bonn's policy, and that now, with control over Eastern Europe re-established, Moscow would be more amenable to making concessions. This division over foreign policy was to provide the main battle ground for the election campaign in 1969 and was to contribute to Brandt's victory.

EXTRA-PARLIAMENTARY OPPOSITION, THE 1969 PRESIDENTIAL ELECTION AND THE END OF THE GRAND COALITION

The formation of the Grand Coalition left the small liberal party, the FDP, as the only and ineffective opposition in parliament and this gave rise to an Extra-Parliamentary Opposition, the APO, made up of intellectuals, students, members of the anti-nuclear lobby etc. There had been disaffection already with the Adenauer government which had burst into the open in 1963 in the so-called 'Spiegel Affair', and Erhard's concept of a 'formed society' had appeared to be uncomfortably close to fascist ideas. Now plans for the passing of emergency laws aroused suspicion. In the eyes of the government these had become necessary for several reasons; every modern state needs provisions for emergencies of all kinds, moreover by passing German legislation certain Allied rights would become obsolete (the Allies were theoretically still entitled to intervene in Germany if democracy there was threatened). However, a broad spectrum of opinion including the trade unions suspected that these laws might be used to curtail civil liberties at home, and loud protests were organized on many occasions. The Grand Coalition inherited this situation which was made worse by the rising tide of student unrest. This was of course an international phenomenon but in Germany it took on a special quality in that the generation conflict focused not only on grievances about educational provisions but also on Germany's recent past. To the students there had never been an adequate debate about the implications of National Socialism in Germany; the past seemed to have been conveniently covered under the blanket of economic prosperity. Student radicalism was strongest in Berlin which over the years had attracted large numbers of radical youths who could avoid military service by residence in the city. In June 1967 violent demonstrations took place against the visit of the Shah of Iran in the course of which a student was killed by the police. In April 1968 the student leader Rudi Dutschke was seriously wounded by a right wing labourer and this started a series of further demonstrations, damage to property, arson – a process which for a section of the APO later culminated in the urban terror of the Baader-Meinhof gang.

Brandt and the SPD were in a difficult position. On the

one hand the APO singled out the SPD as the main trai-
tors who in the Godesberg Programme had abandoned
socialism, who in the Grand Coalition were making
common cause with a former Nazi and who were
supporting the Emergency Laws. The frustration of some
APO members went so far that Brandt was physically
attacked on entering the SPD Conference Hall in Nuremberg in March 1968, an incident which he shrugged off
laconically, the man had not hit him personally 'he has
hit more out of principle'. On the other hand the political
right doubted the party's firmness and reliability when
dealing with the radicals, suspecting them of having
hidden sympathies with them.

The first official party responses to these developments therefore condemned the excesses, including the
attack on Dutschke, and stressed the necessity for law
and order. Brandt as Foreign Secretary singled out the
possible damage to Germany because of the lack of
courtesy shown to the representatives of foreign countries (Berlin University 8 October 1967). For him the APO
was made up of irresponsible political dreamers who
deserved the epitaph 'OPA' (grandfather) more than
APO. He found their appearance at times 'unappetising'.
Moreover, at the SPD Congress in Nuremberg in March
1968 he was reminded of an earlier student radicalism
which had culminated in the burning of books in 1933.
However, Brandt showed greater flexibility towards the
protest movement than other establishment figures,
possibly because he had first hand knowledge through
his son Peter who was closely involved, receiving two
weeks youth custody for participating in an illegal
demonstration. Brandt who had already displeased party
colleagues by his liberal attitude to both his sons (they
had taken part in the filming of Günter Grass's novel 'Cat
and Mouse' with certain provocative shots) was now
called upon to re-assert his paternal authority by send-
ing young Peter abroad – which he refused to do. At

Nuremberg he took a similar position when he stated that to solve the problem by calling upon the authority of the state could not be enough. In January 1969 Brandt addressed an SPD Youth Congress – a flop in terms of 'bridge building' towards the young – at which he reminded the audience that youth had no intrinsic merit, and that only by cooperation could young and old solve society's problems. When in February 1969 the SPD leadership met to discuss the situation in the German universities Brandt saw in the upheavals not only terror and subversion, but 'something which is also not very comfortable, namely an extreme questioning of traditional values and of the established order'. Instead of breaking with the young, the party should try to win over as many of them as possible. This cautious opening coincided with the switch of tactics in the APO, away from open confrontation towards changing society by the 'march through the institutions'. In subsequent years the SPD was transformed by the influx of these young members who, although many settled down to ordinary careers, nevertheless changed the party's traditional complexion. Brandt emerged as their 'hero'; they admired him for his anti-fascist past, for his comparative openness, for his contacts with writers and with the arts, for the tolerance he showed in his family and for his unconventional life style. His obvious discomfort in the Grand Coalition endeared him to them.

The Grand Coalition was rapidly becoming an anachronism. Foreign policy arguments grew more intense after the Soviet invasion of Czechoslovakia. In March 1969 there was a major row over Cambodia's recognition of the GDR. Kiesinger and the CDU had reverted to the Hallstein Doctrine and wanted to break off relations with Cambodia. Brandt was on the brink of resignation. In view of the approaching elections this was not a realistic option but the incident reinforced Brandt's determination to abandon the Grand Coalition as soon as possible and to form a coalition with the liberals instead, should the election results permit it. The first precondition was that the SPD defeat the proposal for the introduction of majority voting at its Nuremberg conference (see above). The FDP on the other hand also underwent changes with the election of a new party chairman, Walter Scheel, who stood more on the left than his predecessor. The party's new programme 'For the Renewal of the Federal Republic' spoke a language similar to that of the SPD. Particularly in foreign affairs the liberals moved closer to the SPD when Scheel proposed the normalization of relations with the GDR, renunciation of the Hallstein Doctrine and acknowledgement of the Oder-Neisse line. However, no open promise of a coalition between the two parties was made at this stage.

A first indication of an impending change in power came with the election of a new president in March 1969. Brandt had put forward a candidate, Gustav Heinemann, who although a former member of the CDU, was acceptable to the FDP because of his liberal conduct as Minister of Justice in the Grand Coalition. Heinemann's nomination turned out to have been a shrewd move for other reasons also; he had been the only establishment figure not to condemn the APO outright, but in a television address after the shooting of Dutschke, had reminded the public not to forget that in a hand which points an accusing finger at others three fingers point back at the accuser, by which he meant that those in authority were not entirely blameless for the surge in discontent among the young. With this attitude Heinemann established himself as the bridge between APO and the government at a crucial time in the history of the FRG, and by backing Heinemann Brandt ranged himself firmly with the progressive elements which later gained him their support.

After his election with the votes of the FDP, Heinemann infuriated the establishment even more by pointing to the significance of his choice as 'a change of power (*Machtwechsel*) [which] has taken place according to the rules of parliamentary democracy.'[4] It was important for the Bonn Republic to experience political change within the framework of the constitution, although the real change would only come after the next elections. These took place in the autumn of 1969 and the position of the SPD was weaker than the proponents of the Grand Coalition in the party had hoped. There had been a string of poor state election results for the SPD with worrying successes for the right wing NPD. In the autumn of 1969 there were a number of unofficial strikes by workers dissatisfied with their share in the benefits of a newly recovered economy.

On the other hand, the Economics Ministry was held by a flamboyant Social Democrat, Professor Schiller. The SPD was not only able to make use of his star qualities in the campaign; his success in restoring economic health to the country spoke for itself. Posters of the time therefore depict Schiller rather more prominently than party leader Brandt who appeared mostly with Schiller. Secondly, the SPD was able to project itself as the progressive party both at home and particularly in foreign policy. At home it demanded far reaching reforms taking on board some of the more reasonable demands put forward by the APO. In this respect the SPD found support among important sections of the media and many intellectuals such as Günter Grass and Heinrich Böll; in 1968 an SPD 'Election Initiative' was set up by writers of the Group 47 who drummed up support for the party in meetings up and down the country. Even more effective, however, was the SPD's record on foreign policy. Brandt could justifiably claim that it had been his pressure which pushed the Grand Coalition into catching up with the stream of international politics; Germany had been led out of its isolation. It was now a question of whether Germany could move forward and play a role in foreign affairs commensurate with the country's economic weight. This implied a continuation of the policy of rapprochement with the east, while remaining firmly rooted in the western system of alliances. Where the CDU stalled and looked back to the apparent certainties of the Adenauer years, the SPD was the party of movement to the future. This projection into a more open future was aided by developments in the international field. In the US Richard Nixon had become President in January 1969 with the avowed intention of ending the war in Vietnam and of improving international links all round, including those with China. The Soviets, now doubly unsettled not only by their own trouble with China (which erupted into open violence on the Ussuri river in March 1969), but also by the prospect of improved US-Chinese relations, became more accommodating in Europe. Where Brandt's previous efforts had met with negative responses, in September 1969 he was invited to Moscow for informal talks.

When the votes were counted it transpired that the gamble of the Grand Coalition had come off for the SPD. The party had increased its share of the votes by 3.4 per cent to 42.7 per cent, although the CDU/CSU suffered only minor losses with 46.1 per cent. The great losers were the NPD who with 4.3 per cent did not get into parliament and the FDP who with 5.8 per cent only just made it. The party had lost two fifths of its electorate by switching to the left without having found a new constituency. However, together SPD and FDP were just strong enough to form a government – a chance which Brandt seized with for him unusual alacrity. Despite his success in Berlin his reputation up to now had been that of being rather indecisive and easily discouraged. He was considered a bad speaker with an often slow and halting delivery; some observers even claimed that he was a man without charisma[5]. The two-time loser in recent elections now imposed his will on Kiesinger and his party colleagues Wehner and Schmidt who would have preferred a continuation of the Grand Coalition. But Brandt was carried forward by the enthusiastic support from ordinary party members.

A watershed in German politics had been reached. For the first time since 1930 a Social Democrat led a German government. As Brandt articulated it on the night of his greatest success so far: 'Now Hitler has truly lost the war'. This gave him the confidence to assert: 'I do not see myself as the Chancellor of a vanquished but of a liberated Germany'. In the short run, more important was the fact that a normal take-over of power had taken place and that with the restoration of a large parliamentary opposition, the APO lost its *raison d'etre*. The SPD in the Grand Coalition had been able to prove that it was able to run large government departments such as Foreign Affairs, Economics and Defence perfectly successfully, that it had a team of competent men, and that it had more constructive ideas about the future. The CDU on the other hand had emerged as exhausted after twenty years in power. It now had to learn to live in opposition.

The Chancellor, 1969–74

4

THE FIRST BRANDT/SCHEEL CABINET (1969–72)

It was mainly on the basis of their outlook on foreign policy that the new coalition between SPD and FDP was formed. Their negotiations proceeded speedily with the FDP accepting three ministries (Foreign – for party leader Scheel, Interior and Agriculture). But the coalition was nevertheless highly controversial particularly in the FDP, and Brandt was elected Chancellor by only two votes (251:249). Although this was two votes more than Adenauer had obtained in 1949, as Brandt was quick to point out, it also reflected the shaky ground on which the new government rested. This partly explains the enormous speed with which it tackled the tasks it had set itself.

Brandt's opening speech to parliament was both a ringing declaration of a new beginning and a commitment to continuity for Germany. In internal affairs Brandt announced a whole range of reforms (education, tax, administration, law etc.) and provocatively distanced himself from previous regimes: 'We do not stand at the end of our democracy, we are only just beginning'.[1]

73

Moreover, echoing the views of the young, he demanded that Germany should 'dare more democracy' and thus become a modern, forward looking state and a fairer society. In foreign policy on the other hand the government announced continuity. Although it was prepared to sign the nuclear Non-Proliferation Treaty (which had been a divisive issue in the Grand Coalition) its intentions were a continuation of the opening to the east in general and an extension of the renunciation of the use of force to the GDR and further improvements in relations with it.

This first speech as Chancellor was a piece of brilliant rhetoric, a manifesto of a 'new dawn' and full of 'infectious moral and participatory passion'. Couched in terms of modern social science it signalled very high and far reaching objectives. However, these soon came up against political and economic realities, and the exaggerated expectations which Brandt had aroused in his followers and the German population at large partly explain their equally exaggerated disappointment when developments fell short of what had been promised. There were three areas which preoccupied the first Brandt/Scheel government: *Ostpolitik*, and in the domestic sphere, the economy and internal security.

Ostpolitik

In his opening declaration Brandt had accepted the existence of 'two states in Germany' and although their relations to each other would always be special, he nevertheless went a step further towards a fulfilment of the GDR's objective, its recognition as a sovereign state. Moreover, with the signing of the Non-Proliferation Treaty in November 1969 which the Soviets had desired for some time, the new government signalled its preparedness to make further concessions and its hope that in a thus improved general atmosphere constructive developments might take place. Indeed, the unsuccessful moves by the Grand Coalition had shown that an improvement in the relations with the USSR were the precondition for any progress in the contacts with other East European states. It was Brandt's good fortune that this found a ready response in the Soviet Union where General Secretary Brezhnev was keen to counterbalance his troublesome eastern flank with peace in Europe. Moreover, he was keen on improved economic coopera- tion with West Germany and hoped to wean her away from her traditional close integration with the west. Brandt, on the other hand, had revealed his determina- tion to act with greater independence in international affairs, notably from the US. For these reasons Brandt soon emerged as Brezhnev's favourite partner in western Europe (to the chagrin of the French and the irritation of the Americans – see below), and this explains the compa- ratively rapid progress in German-Soviet relations, albeit after tough negotiations.

The objective of *Ostpolitik* was improved relations with all east European states and the winning for Germany of greater foreign policy mobility while remaining firmly rooted in the western alliance. There were four accords to be negotiated: with Moscow (crucial for the rest), Poland, the GDR and as an all-embracing international guarantee for the other arrangements, a Four Power Agreement on Berlin. A further treaty with Czechoslovakia followed later, in December 1973.

The Moscow Treaty

The talks with Moscow began as early as 8 December 1969 and from January 1970 were conducted by Brandt's special advisor Egon Bahr. There was moreover a secret direct channel of communications between Brandt and Brezhnev by which they could exchange their views personally and unconventionally. There were three rounds of talks concerned with the mutual renunciation of the use of force and the recognition of the existing borders, including the Oder–Neisse line which formed the western frontier of Poland, and of the border between the FRG and GDR. Both parties gave the assurance that they had no territorial claims against anyone and no desire to make such claims in the future; normalization in Europe had to build on the realities created by World War II. In a second part the FRG declared its intention of negotiating relevant treaties with Poland, Czechoslovakia and the GDR and that these treaties should form a unit together with that to be concluded with Moscow. Although the FRG did not recognize the GDR diplomatically she undertook to conclude a treaty which would have the same status as that between the FRG and the USSR, or the GDR with third countries. The FRG also committed itself to work towards the acceptance into the United Nations of both German states. Moreover, the FRG agreed that the GDR could now be recognized by the western states, thus officially abandoning the Hallstein Doctrine. Both sides agreed on the desirability of a Europe-wide security conference.

In June the draft agreement of ten points was leaked to the German press (the so-called 'Bahr Paper') and caused a storm of protest from the opposition and from sections of the public at large: Bahr had negotiated without formal instructions from the cabinet; Brandt had made too many concessions without concrete results in return ('a sell-out of German interests'; Brandt was a 'renunciation politician'). Although this premature publication prevented the Soviet concessions which the opposition desired – the Soviets could hardly give in to open German pressure – it allowed the delegation in subsequent negotiations to insist on a satisfactory conclusion of the Berlin negotiations prior to acceptance of the Moscow Treaty by the *Bundestag* (the *Berlin Junktim*). Furthermore, the Germans handed the Soviets a 'Letter about German Unity' in which it was stated that the treaty did not contradict the German aim to work towards peace in Europe, in which the German people would regain their unity in free self determination. On this basis Brandt and Brezhnev signed the Moscow Treaty on 12 August 1970. The treaty thus kept the question of German re-unification open. The Brandt/Scheel government pursued the same aim with the western powers with an exchange of notes in which the western Allies accepted that in the view of both partners to the Moscow Treaty, the rights and responsibilities of all four powers for Germany and for Berlin were not affected by the treaty.

The Warsaw Treaty

Negotiations with Poland began on 3 February 1970 and ran parallel with those in Moscow. Indeed, the Warsaw talks started on a wrong note because the discussions in Moscow on the Polish border question had gone over the heads of the Poles and had ignored Polish national sovereignty. Again Brandt involved himself directly with letters to the Polish state and party leadership. There were three important problems, the FRG's recognition of the Oder–Neisse line, the transfer of Germans and those of German origins from Poland and economic relations. Widely differing views had to be overcome, although on the border question the Germans were prepared to meet Polish demands. Closely connected with it, however, was the status of those Germans who had either been driven from their homeland or who had stayed behind in Poland. The Germans considered the expulsion of millions of their compatriots as a crime and demanded for the Germans in Poland the status of a national minority. The Poles considered the 'transfer' of the Germans as covered by the Potsdam Conference and those Germans inside Poland as Polish nationals. Further discrepancies existed about compensation for crimes against humanity committed by the Germans during the war. The Federal government did not deny its obligations but insisted on involving the GDR in this compensation and on paying it to the families of individual victims; it pointed to the vast territories which the Poles had taken over at the end of the war as sufficient general compensation. Despite these sensitive issues agreement was speedily reached. It was during Brandt's visit to Warsaw for the signature on 7 December 1970 that the now famous 'kneeling of Warsaw' incident occurred when he fell to his knees after placing a wreath on a memorial for the murdered Jews of the Warsaw ghetto. It was the gesture which expressed what words could not say adequately, the acceptance of guilt and the sorrow for unspeakable crimes committed by Germans against millions of innocent people. This gesture captured the imagination of the world and did a great deal to restore respect for Germany. It singled Brandt out as a politician with a moral dimension which had been lacking in his predecessors, and it was this link between politics and morality which made him popular with the young and progressive elements in Germany. However, a survey revealed that overall only 41 per cent of Germans thought the gesture appropriate, 48 per cent thought it exaggerated, and among 30–60 years old 54 per cent rejected it.[2]

Although there was agreement on the Oder–Neisse line as Poland's western border, on the question of the transfer of German people from Poland, the treaty remained vague. Indeed, the Polish government after the change from Gomulka to Gierek handled the exit permits for Germans in Poland in a restrictive way, and in 1975, after Brandt's resignation, an additional agreement had to be negotiated. More than in the Moscow Treaty Brandt had given a lot but had received less and gave ammunition to a prolonged and resentful opposition in Germany. The Polish treaty thus lacked balance. However, for Brandt it seemed more important that a process of normalization in the relations between the two states had begun on which later more practical agreements could be built.

Negotiations with the GDR

Although Brandt had offered negotiations to the GDR in his opening statement to parliament he had in fact, as with Poland, come to a general agreement with the Soviets first in the belief that they could be used as a lever to force the recalcitrant East Germans to move towards the West German position. That his calculation was correct was explicitly confirmed by Gromyko on 10 March 1970; when the East German leader Ulbricht proved to be an obstacle he was forced to resign on 3 July 1971. The fact that, despite this high level German–Soviet understanding, contacts between Brandt and Stoph (the East German Minister-President) still took place was due mainly to the realization that the East Germans would try to mobilize eastern bloc feelings against Bonn and that a show of goodwill would strengthen Bonn's position. Two meetings therefore took place: Brandt visited Stoph in Erfurt (19 March 1970) and the latter returned the visit in Kassel (21 May 1970). It was the first time that a West German Chancellor had visited the GDR and negotiated with his counterpart on an equal footing. Moreover, the tumultuous welcome which the population gave him despite all official efforts to hold the crowds back demonstrated the longing for unity of ordinary East Germans. The image of Brandt trying from his hotel window to calm the crowds in Erfurt also received world-wide publicity. For Brandt they demonstrated that German unity was not a fiction but reality and that to work towards German unification was a realistic policy. However, the second meeting at Kassel also showed that this unity was not to be achieved in the near future. There was a fruitless stating of their respective positions after which both sides agreed to postpone further contacts during a pause for reflection (*Denkpause*).

Four Power Negotiations over Berlin

In these discussions between the ambassadors of the four victorious powers in World War II the western powers sought from the Soviets a guarantee of the existing situation in Berlin. This would remove the recurrent threats to the status of the city and to its links with West Germany which had bedevilled it in the past, and of which Brandt as its mayor in the days of the construction of the Wall was particularly aware. Moreover, it would have the advantage in western eyes of making the Soviets rather than the East Germans responsible for the adherence to the agreement. For those very reasons neither Soviets nor East Germans were particularly keen to proceed and the negotiations stalled throughout 1970. A breakthrough came in the early summer of 1971 when Ulbricht left office and Nixon announced his impending visit to China in June. This made the Soviets keener on cooperation in Europe, and as the Berlin agreement was now a precondition for the acceptance by the FRG of the Moscow Treaty, it led to a softening of the eastern position on Berlin. The previously awkward problem of Berlin's legal status ('Greater Berlin' or only 'West-Berlin') was simply excluded, and Berlin was referred to as the 'relevant area' which both sides could interpret as they wished. The agreement came in three 'layers' with the Four Power Agreement as the base, special accords between the FRG and the Senate of West Berlin with the GDR, and thirdly, by a special Four Power Protocol. The Four Power Agreement was signed on 3 September 1971; a number of technical accords such as that on transit or the arrangements concerning visits by West Berliners to East Berlin and the GDR, were concluded in December 1971. With the protocol the Soviet Union accepted the *de facto* integration of West Berlin into the economic, social and legal order of the Federal Republic although the nature of this integration remained in dispute: the western allies spoke vaguely of 'ties' or 'liens'. What really mattered to the West Germans, however, was the fact that the *East* German view of West Berlin as an independent political unit had been rejected. With the Four Power Agreement on Berlin the *Ostpolitik* package was complete. Subsequently there were further formal treaties between the FRG and the GDR such as that for the regulation of traffic between the two Germanies and Berlin (26 May 1972), and the more fundamental Basic Treaty (*Grundlagenvertrag*) between FRG and GDR. The latter was concluded only in December 1972; in it the FRG recognized the GDR as an equal and independent state and accepted that the two German states should be represented in the UN. However, the acceptance of the package was by no means a foregone conclusion and took place only after momentous battles inside the FRG. For Brandt the importance of the package was that it served peace and was directed towards the future. But there were also tangible, albeit small, short term results such as when in the new manuals issued to Soviet troops the FRG was no longer singled out as aggressor, or that the FRG was not made the scapegoat for the unrest in Poland in the early 1970s as had been the case previously.

Brandt meanwhile rode on the crest of his spectacular popularity with the Soviet leader Brezhnev with whom he spent three days at Oreaga on the Crimea in September 1971. All in all they had sixteen hours of informal talks (and a thorough test of Brandt's *Trinkfestigkeit*, his ability to drink, which he passed with ease); never before had a German Chancellor had such extensive contact with a Soviet leader. Brandt has maintained good relations with the Kremlin to the present day. Brandt saw in these direct German/Soviet contacts a 'limited bilateralism' which demonstrated again the greater independence of the FRG in international affairs. From this it followed that although no concrete new policy initiatives were developed, a confidence building exchange of views

over a range of issues took place. In view of the still
unratified treaties this was a useful exercise and the
Soviet leader made it clear that Moscow would only
honour the Berlin arrangements if Bonn accepted the
Moscow Treaty (the so-called *Counter-Junktim*). More
important however, were the wider discussions which,
although they covered actual problems such as China,
seemed to focus on the future of détente in Europe,
where Brandt saw a 'mutual interest' between the USSR
and the FRG in the reduction of troops and armaments.
The first phase of *Ostpolitik*, the signing of the treaties,
should be followed by a phase of military détente
embracing the whole of Europe, in which the existing bi-
lateral contacts would be widened to a multi-lateral
approach such as that of the MBFR or CSCE conferences.
Nothing less than the creation of new security structures
in central Europe was envisaged. The immense implications for Germany were obvious and subsequently the
Brandt/Scheel government persistently pushed for the
holding of Europe-wide conferences. However, the actual
decisions to hold these conferences were made by Nixon
and Brezhnev (Moscow, May 1972) – a timely reminder
of the limited real power of the FRG. Nevertheless, the
significance of Oreaga lies in the fact that a Europe-wide
perspective was developed and that negotiations seemed
nearer, which went beyond the settling of old, post World
War II scores in the direction of a new European order.
However, reactions in the US were lukewarm and another
twenty years were to pass before the vision of Oreaga
could approach reality.

In December 1971 Brandt reached a pinnacle of international acclaim when he was awarded the Nobel Peace
Prize, the first post-war German to be so honoured. It
was a symbol of West Germany's gradual international
rehabilitation to which Brandt, next to Adenauer, had
made the greatest contribution. However, international
honours did not help much when it came to fighting the

many domestic battles over *Ostpolitik*, the economy, the problems of internal security and in the SPD. The climax came in April 1972 with the parliamentary opposition's attempt to overthrow the Brandt/Scheel government.

Domestic Conflicts

The Economy

The first Brandt/Scheel cabinet had three Finance Ministers in three years, a reflection of the turbulence of the time, although the main shock, the oil crisis was still to come (Autumn, 1973). The German economy had recovered quickly from the mild recession of the mid-60s; however inflation had risen faster than growth and in 1972 stood at 6 per cent. Although industrial output had increased annually unemployment had also risen; Germany was suffering from the phenomenon of 'stagflation'. These figures however need to be seen in perspective: in 1975 Germany's inflation rate was still 6 per cent as against 9.1 per cent in the USA, 11.8 per cent in Japan and France and 24.2 per cent in the UK.[3] The problem facing the government was that a solution to both unemployment *and* inflation was not possible. Forced to make a choice, and in view of its ambitious reform programme the government opted for 'deficit spending', and Minister of Finance, Möller, resigned in May 1971. His portfolio was taken over by Schiller who thus combined it with his own Ministry of Economics in one 'super ministry'. Schiller, flattered in his considerable vanity, overlooked the inherent contradictions between the two jobs, but Brandt with complete personal confidence in Schiller's abilities and with limited personal interest in the problems involved, could not overcome the intense personality clashes which erupted between Schiller and the ambitious Schmidt over proposed cuts in the budget of the Ministry of Defence. Brandt more than once left cabinet sessions when their feuding got out of control, and even thought of resignation. Brandt's style in cabinet was one of debate leading to ultimate consensus; he abhorred decisions reached by voting. This failure to impose his authority on his colleagues gravely weakened his position. Rather than backing Schiller whose economic advice was sound (but who had meanwhile also fallen foul of the left wing of the SPD and whose vanity was hard to stomach) he reluctantly allowed his resignation. Ironically Schmidt, who became the new 'super-minister', forced through many of Schiller's measures which he himself had previously opposed. With his know-how and relentless ambition he showed up Brandt as comparatively weak and indecisive. He thus grew into the role of Crown Prince and became a direct threat to the Chancellor. Brandt, on the other hand, did nothing to stop him and this neglect, or perhaps naive faith in the loyalty of his colleagues was to cost him dear later.

Internal security

Since 1970 the control of terrorism which had its roots in the student unrest of 1968/69 became a dominant concern of public opinion. It was difficult to explain a phenomenon whose leaders were often intellectuals from comfortable middle class homes. One explanation was that students who succeeded comparatively easily in disrupting the traditional workings of the universities were frustrated in their wider demands for changes in society as a whole. Their solution was terrorism: urban guerilla activities would alert the intimidated masses to the suppression and manipulation they suffered at the hands of the authorities and the media, and they would thus be encouraged to shake off their shackles. However, a series of arsons, robberies and murders, notably of judges and particularly the international extension of terrorism as illustrated by the murder of Israeli sportsmen in their rooms during the Olympic Games at

Munich, had the reverse effect; an intense search began for the right response by which the state could protect its citizens without endangering their basic civil liberties. However, up to the summer of 1972 the state conveyed an image of comparative helplessness mainly because the issue was complicated by the problem of sympathizers, a group of several thousand active and a much wider network of passive supporters who, so it was claimed, provided a generally supportive atmosphere in which terrorists could flourish. A dangerous situation was opening for the Brandt government as the right aligned itself with 'Law and Order' and everything to the left could conveniently be labelled 'sympathizers'. This had two consequences: it prevented a rational debate and it pushed Brandt far more in the direction of the authoritarian use of state power. An example for the former was provided by Heinrich Böll's article in the *Spiegel* of January 1972, in which he castigated the foul language and unobjective reporting by right wing papers, pleading for mercy for the terrorists – which turned him temporarily into a social outcast. Brandt's nervousness over the whole issue was increased by the fact that owing to his eastern contacts he was already being labelled as unreliable; this was made worse by the radical and vociferous veering to the left of the Young Socialists, the Jusos (see below). In order not to endanger *Ostpolitik* Brandt and the SPD worked hard to distance themselves from communists and other irresponsible leftists and to represent the SPD as a moderate, responsible party and Brandt himself as heading a strong government. Thus Brandt and Wehner prevented President Heinemann from making a speech which seemed too 'humane' and thus soft on terrorists. On 4 February 1972 Brandt himself addressed the nation on TV sharply condemning all terrorism and its sympathizers, while also rejecting the blind hitting-out of the police. It is in this light that the notorious 'Extremists Decision' of 28 January 1972 has to be seen. This concerned the employment of members of radical organizations in the civil service. There were two problems. Firstly, the German civil service is much wider than, say, the British government service, and comprises all state employees down to postmen and railway officials; any legislation would thus affect a vast number of people whose political opinions would not endanger the state. Secondly, there was the membership of radical albeit legal organizations such as the DKP, the German Communist party which was refounded in 1969. The Extremists Decision (or *Radikalenerlass* as it was also known) was not new legislation: it built on the existing Civil Service Laws of 1953 and 1957. But its later use, notably in states governed by the CDU, gave cause for concern, particularly as the authorities had the right to investigate any applicant. It was this rather than the actual exclusion of activists, whose numbers remained comparatively small, which raised fears as to the government's commitment to democratic freedom. Brandt later distanced himself from the Decision but found that, owing to the FRG's federal structure it was far more difficult to undo legislation than to introduce it. In the short run, however, the Decision had a positive effect; it showed that the government was 'taking action' which, together with the restructuring of the police, the extension of secret surveillance and the capture of leading members of the terrorists' groups gave Brandt an excellent platform from which to conduct the subsequent election campaign.

The 'Constructive Vote of Non-Confidence' and the Elections of November 1972

Brandt's attitude to internal security was partly shaped by the continuous erosion of his majority in parliament where, despite or because of the international recognition, his foreign policy came in for ferocious opposition. It was not only that Brandt seemed to have given up too much of Germany's national interest without receiving concrete concessions in return – to some extent perhaps a valid criticism; there was unease with the general course of the government which a comparatively moderate CDU member like the former Foreign Secretary Gerhard Schröder described as showing 'a fatal drift to the Left'.[4] There had been a steady trickle of defections from conservatives in the FDP, and in the spring of 1972 four members of the SPD left the coalition which reduced the coalition's majority to four. With more defections possible, the fate of *Ostpolitik* was in the balance. However, as the CDU was increasing in strength and in April achieved an absolute majority in the state elections of Baden-Württemberg, its leader, Rainer Barzel, felt encouraged to launch an all-out attack on Brandt and attempt to unseat his government by the so-called 'Constructive Vote of Non-Confidence'. As a reaction to the ease with which governments had been overthrown during the Weimar Republic, the constitution of the FRG had made a change of government other than after an election much more difficult. Article 67 of the Basic Law prescribed that not only did the opposition need a majority against the incumbent government, this needed to be 'constructive' in that there also needed to be a majority for a successor government. In April 1972 Barzel was confident that enough members of the coalition would vote both against Brandt and for him.

Although this was an entirely legal procedure the population at large saw it as a manipulation of the voters' decision of less than three years earlier, and as an attempt by the over-ambitious Barzel to gain power by less than respectable means. Indeed, there was a ground-swell of popular indignation with widespread demon-strations and work stoppages; there was even talk of a general strike should the vote go against Brandt. History, i.e. the end of the Weimar Republic by parliamentary manoeuvring, seemed to be repeating itself; this time the democratic forces in the country were not going to submit without a fight. Excitement was no less inside parliament with intense speculation about the loyalty of individual MPs and rumours of votes being 'bought' by bribery. On the day even mortally ill members were wheeled out to take part. When the votes were counted the unexpected had happened: Barzel won only 247 instead of the 249 he needed to succeed; his calculation had misfired and Brandt had won the day. The public, glued to TV sets and radios rejoiced, justice seemed to have been done. Brandt recollects that he had not been certain of success but that he had awaited the outcome of the vote 'with greater calm than many assumed ... I did not exclude [the possibility] that a few prominent members of the CDU would abandon their [own] candidate'.[5] In subsequent years there have been several revelations of 'dirty deals' behind the scenes but the exact details have not yet been cleared up.

The tight vote revealed that the government's position was as shaky as ever and new elections were necessary in order to produce a more workable majority. These were eventually fixed for 19 November, after the safe passage through parliament of the *Ostpolitik* treaties, which Brandt had not wished to become the subject of the election campaign. The voters were asked to endorse the overall direction of German foreign policy as well as that of the planned domestic reforms (see below). As such the elections produced a much sharper commitment to one or the other of the political camps with a display of buttons, stickers and posters not previously seen in German politics. Indeed, the campaign unleashed high political passions; political opinions were polarized to an unheard-of degree with the involvement of journalists, artists and intellectuals for Brandt while industrialists spent a fortune on advertising for the CDU. They could not match the emotional campaign waged by the pro-Brandt camp: Brandt was portrayed as the 'moral politician' who symbolized the union of power and intellect. He was presented as the great international statesman who as Nobel Prize winner had brought recognition to Germany. Brandt himself reached new heights of charismatic leadership; election meetings had almost religious overtones: 'Willy Brandt can transform election meetings into religious celebrations. He talks almost always largo ... his hands stretched out in a searching gesture, asking for "compassion" ...' Other observers noted that his intonation had the 'sublime monotony of Gregorian chant'.[6] Brandt's style, the soft method of 'soul massage', was successful in creating a very special, emotional atmosphere; older women tried to touch him 'with tears in their eyes and to push rosaries and amulets into his hands'. Younger women simply adored him. Against his veneration attempts by the opposition to revive the personal smear campaigns against him with references to his illegitimate birth or to the SPD as a 'harem's party' simply backfired on the accusers. The mobilization of public opinion was reflected in the extremely high turnout for democratic elections of 91.17 per cent. The SPD with a gain of three million votes achieved the best result in its history and with 45.8 per cent became the largest party in Germany. The CDU/CSU had also profited from the higher poll with an increase of 1.6 million votes (44.9 per cent). With gains of 1.2 million votes (8.4 per cent) the result was particularly comforting for the FDP which was recovering from its trough of the late 1960s and was gaining a new profile as the party which was going to moderate the more extreme reformist zeal of the SPD. Above all, it was an enormous personal triumph for Willy Brandt, it was a ringing public endorsement of his *Ostpolitik* and of his person as Chancellor. Moreover, he had found a new electoral 'home' for the SPD which in addition to the traditional support from the workers had found support in the new middle class of leading employees, civil servants, independent business men and also among the new young voters, over 60 per cent of whom had opted for the SPD. However, this electoral basis was fragile and volatile, their often mutually exclusive political objectives being bridged for the time only by foreign policy triumphs and the personality of the Chancellor.

THE SECOND BRANDT/SCHEEL CABINET (1972-4)

Although the government now had a much healthier parliamentary basis (230 SPD, 41 FDP against 225 CDU/CSU) its freedom of action was nevertheless circumscribed by the majority for the opposition in the Upper House, the *Bundesrat*, which represented the states and could delay and often obstruct controversial legislation. This became particularly relevant for the government's programme of internal reforms which was severely affected by the oil and dollar crises. Where much of government planning had been carried out on the assumption of continuous economic growth these notions were now challenged, as was shown in the study carried out on behalf of the seven leading industrial nations (the so-called 'Club of Rome'), 'The Limits of Growth' which was published in the autumn of 1972. Moreover, encouraged by the SPD's resounding election success the Left in the party became more assertive and made public statements which harmed the party's image; Brandt had to use all his authority to keep them within the overall party line. In addition, German workers now demanded their share in Germany's new prosperity which culminated in a series of inflationary wage settlements and for the government particularly embarrassing public sector strikes. Brandt also suffered disillusionment in foreign policy where the eastern bloc was far from fulfilling its side of the *Ostpolitik* bargain and where

Brandt's *Westpolitik* came up against a determined and critical American president.

The Formation of the Government

One of the reasons for Brandt's 'largo' delivery of election speeches was chronic laryngitis which was aggravated by the continuous stress on his vocal cords during the campaign. Immediately after victory was achieved he had to go into hospital for an operation and was out of action for several weeks. The doctors allowed him only ten minutes talking time a day and imposed a ban on smoking – a severe blow for the normally chain smoking Brandt. Moreover, the overall exhaustion contributed to another attack of depression from which Brandt despite his resounding victory seemed to extricate himself with greater difficulty than on previous occasions. On the other hand the important matter of the formation of the new cabinet needed to be settled and although the general outlines had been agreed before Brandt went into hospital there was enough scope for his colleagues Schmidt and Wehner to show less than complete loyalty to Brandt when they negotiated the posts of the new cabinet without consulting the Chancellor. But Brandt allowed this to happen by not confronting them openly from hospital. Thus the FDP was able to win five ministries; since the names were published in the press the incensed Brandt was left no choice other than to accept the situation. In addition, there was the replacement of the SPD government spokesman by a member of the FDP although Brandt found him personally likeable and hence acceptable. Other personnel changes were in the long run more damaging for Brandt: the dynamic head of the Chancellery, Ehmke, Brandt's close adviser and friend was replaced by a bureaucratic nonentity. Ehmke had forced Brandt to face issues and make decisions, but the new team was more prepared to pander to his contemplative moods. Thus a process began whereby unpleasant facts were kept from the Chancellor who grew more remote and increasingly less decisive. The spokesman was often not sufficiently informed to enable him to project government policies favourably to the outside world and threatened to resign; Brandt also became even less decisive in cabinet where gossiping and lack of discipline increased alarmingly.

This went hand in hand with the government's continued claim to represent new political values: these were highlighted in Brandt's opening statement to parliament at the beginning of his second term of office in the use of terms like 'quality of life', *Heimat*, *Geborgenheit* (homeliness), 'humanity'. Although this speech was less wide ranging in scope than that in 1969 and there were fewer, more realistic objectives presented in order of priority, the expectations of the public which had voted Brandt into office remained extremely high – which helps to explain his swift fall from power when these hopes could not be fulfilled.

Problems of domestic policies

Although Brandt's preoccupation with *Ostpolitik* was obvious he had in fact, on coming to power, seen his main aim, in line with old Social Democratic traditions, as introducing reforms into Germany and modernizing German society. This part of his government programme was therefore tackled simultaneously with his foreign policy initiatives, but progress proved much slower and some projects came to fruition only after Brandt left office; some did not succeed at all. Moreover, some projects such as the reform of the legal system simply continued reform programmes of the previous government; others such as the reform of the Social Services, the widening of Co-Determination in industry, or the planned reform of the education system carried on already ongoing debates; as early as the mid-1960s specialists had talked of Germany's educational 'catastrophe' and the sociologist, Ralf Dehrendorf had demanded 'education as a civic right'. However, what the Brandt/Scheel governments provided was immense impetus, stimulation of public debate and speedy action where this could be done without controversy. Thus in June 1970 the right to vote was lowered to 18 and the right to stand as a candidate was brought down to 21 – measures which paid off handsomely for the government in the 1972 campaign. In 1973 the age of majority was lowered from 21 to 18 years. However, in the question of Co-Determination the interests of the two coalition partners clashed directly, and the trade unions did not succeed in extending the model of the Coal and Steel industry – equal representation for workers on the board – to the rest of industry.

Even more controversial was the reform of §218 of the German Penal Code which since 1871 had punished abortion with strict imprisonment (*Zuchthaus*). This time public opinion was more directly involved because the heavy guns of the Catholic Church were uncompromisingly directed against any change. This meant that the CDU and the CDU-controlled states were so adamantly opposed that they fought the proposal at every stage, not merely unwilling to accept the vote in favour in parliament (5 June 1974), but challenging in the Constitutional Court the subsequent new law which the president promulgated on the basis of this vote. The result was that in CDU/CSU controlled states it remained almost impossible to obtain a legal abortion, a situation which has not changed up to the present day. In education a restructuring of the universities was achieved, with some powers removed from the traditionally all-powerful professors and a tightening of academic courses. The school debate raged on for many more years and also ended in different practices for SPD and CDU governed states, with the former often adopting some form of comprehensive system and the latter mainly sticking to the old grammar schools.

On balance the reform programme of the Brandt and Scheel government was a positive achievement. However, in the wake of the oil crisis the public mood turned away from the idea of reform as such; a *Werte wandel* (change of values) was taking place whereby reforms tended to be equated with careless expenditure and lack of realism. Brandt for the time being remained under pressure to 'deliver' particularly inside the SPD but also among the 'progressive' public at large. Thus he had difficulty in controlling the Young Socialists (*Jusos*) whom he had repeatedly admonished to show greater realism in their demands and greater consideration for the party's public image; in March 1973 he threatened to resign to stem the flood of internal opposition which was undermining the party's unity. But the fact that Brandt needed such a big stick to keep the party in order also reflected his weakening grip on affairs, and this impression was reinforced in the public at large by the go-slow of air traffic controllers from May to November 1973, which paralysed much of Germany's air traffic during the psychologically important summer months. Later in 1973 the Federal Republic along with other states in the western world suffered the shock of the drastic rise in oil prices but the government did not really manage to convey the world wide nature of the crisis; when Brandt imposed speed limits and a ban on Sunday driving these measures seemed to be a hasty overreaction by the government.

Two further incidents served to reduce his prestige, the strike by public service employees and the 'Steiner/ Wienand Affair' which was labelled the 'Watergate of Bonn'. Throughout 1973 there had been inflationary wage settlements, but in view of the oil crisis it seemed of the utmost importance that inflation be kept under control with wage rises under 10 per cent. However, despite Brandt's personal appeals, public employees started strike action whereupon local government employers caved in fairly rapidly, leaving Brandt little option but to give in as well, which made him appear 'soft'. The 'Steiner/Wienand Affair' referred to allegations of vote rigging during the attempt to topple Brandt in April 1972. A public enquiry from 15 June 1973 to 27 March 1974 confirmed what everyone suspected anyway, dirty deals had been done by all concerned (although the last details were again not uncovered). However, the discrepancy between the government's high moral tone and the shabby reality of political infighting reflected adversely on Brandt.

Foreign Policy

By the time Brandt's second cabinet was in place the last treaty of the *Ostpolitik* 'package', the Basic Treaty with the GDR, was concluded. The two German states established 'normal' relations with each other, although they stopped short of diplomatic recognition and only exchanged *Chargés d'Affairs* instead of ambassadors. In September 1973 both Germanies were accepted into the UN. A more tangible result for the German population was the improvement of contacts with the GDR; the number of visits from West Germany and West Berlin to the GDR rose to 6.9 million in 1972 and 8 million in 1973. The telephone network which had broken down completely between West Berlin, East Berlin and the GDR in 1969 was restored and the control of transit traffic from West Germany to West Berlin speeded up. But there were also grave setbacks: in November 1973 the East Germans increased the amount of money which West German visitors had to exchange into East German currency from DM 5.— to DM 10.— for a day and from DM 10.— to DM 20.— for a longer visit. They also tried to prevent the West Germans from establishing their new Environment Ministry in Berlin in January 1974 and ostentatiously reinforced their western 'state border'. In October 1974 the new GDR constitution eradicated all references to the continued existence of a 'German nation'. Brandt appealed in a letter to Brezhnev (30 December 1973) to put pressure on the East Germans to act in the new spirit of *Ostpolitik* and even asked President Nixon to intercede with the Soviets in this matter. It was clear that despite *Ostpolitik* the superpowers still called the tune in German affairs.

There were also difficulties with other aspects of the policy, such as the negotiations with Czechoslovakia which were getting bogged down over the problem of the German renunciation of the Munich Agreement of 1938. *Ostpolitik* had lost much of its élan. At the same time there were difficulties in the west, both in Europe and in the relations with the USA. Although Brandt stressed repeatedly that it was the FRG's intention to 'Europeanize' the process of détente between the superpowers, and that *Ostpolitik* was only possible in the context of Germany's firm integration in the west, there was distrust of the Germans in the other European countries where it was feared that nationalist tendencies were raising their heads again in Germany. It was therefore with some glee that the French prevented an official German translation of the Berlin Treaty. Relations with the Americans became cooler in the wake of the dollar and oil crises. There was irritation in the White House with Brandt's more independently 'German' stance. Even the preparedness of the Brandt government to take on a larger proportion of the cost of stationing US troops – a by now traditional bone of contention between the US and the FRG – did not improve matters. In the eyes of the Americans Brandt's more independent policies had given fresh impetus for new initiatives to European cooperation; in the summer of 1972 this had been formalized

with the setting up of EPC (European Political Cooperation), to supplement the primarily economic orientation of the EC. However, while France saw this as a means by which Europe could coordinate its views and present the outside world, notably the US, with a joint position, Brandt advocated a regular European/American dialogue which would help the Europeans to formulate a joint view. He saw the US/EC relationship as an 'organic link' between equals but even this conciliatory formula was unacceptable to the Americans. Ironically the latter had declared 1973 'Europe Year' but they opposed European attempts to define their common identity such as the 'Copenhagen Declaration' (September 1973) and saw in European aims for 'bi-lateral' external relations a provocation.

Brandt, caught in the tension between Europe, and more specifically France, and the US tried to follow a policy of even-handedness (*sowohl-als-auch*), an approach which became particularly difficult to sustain in the Near East. On the one hand he seemed to be close to the Soviet line on the Middle-East conflict (solution by the involvement of the two superpowers; greater flexibility on Arab interests), as discussed with Brezhnev during the latter's return visit to Germany in May 1973. On the other Brandt went to Israel in June 1973 as the first German Chancellor to visit the country, thus making an important contribution to Jewish/German reconciliation. Once the Yom Kippur war broke out Brandt's position became even more complicated, with the US insisting on using German bases for the supply of the Israelis which Brandt refused along with the other European governments, although the shipment of US equipment from Bremerhaven to Israel was carried out without consultation with the German government, and was stopped only after an outcry in the German press. Brandt attempted to establish a link between the interested parties, including the superpowers, but refused to act directly as a mediator between Arabs and Israelis. As a result both the US and the Israelis saw him as dangerously pro-Arab. Moreover, President Nixon openly accused Brandt that his 'softness' towards the Arabs was an attempt to safeguard his *Ostpolitik* by supporting the Soviet Union in the Near East. The subsequent oil crisis produced prolonged wrangling between the Europeans and the Americans with the latter determined not to allow an independent European stance vis-à-vis the oil producers; they even threatened the withdrawal of Europe's security 'shield' if the Europeans broke ranks (with serious consequences for Israel). Brandt's attempts at even-handedness were also caught in the growing conflict between the French and the Americans; the latter used Germany's greater vulnerability to apply pressure on the Europeans. Faced with a choice the Germans had to opt for continued US support. It was no accident that it was while the Germans chaired the EPC meetings in the first half of 1974 that a formula was found which gave the US the right to be consulted in the EPC decision making process (the Gymnich Formula, 20/21 April

1974). As with *Ostpolitik*, so also the real power situation in the west showed up the limited freedom of action which the Germans (and Europeans) possessed.

The Resignation

Brandt's potential influence as mediator in the Franco-American conflict was weakened by growing criticism of his leadership inside Germany. This was all the more damning as it came from his most important colleagues, Schmidt and Wehner; Wehner's was actually made during an interview in Moscow where he headed a visiting group of German parliamentarians, while Brandt was in New York in connection with the Germans' entry into the UN. The way Brandt handled this open challenge was indicative of his weaknesses and anticipated his later resignation. Although he was profoundly angered and hurt, these sentiments did not lead to drastic action such as the sacking of Wehner which would have been necessary to restore Brandt's authority. Instead Brandt accepted Wehner's apologies, a personal showdown was not in his nature. There may also have been some doubt in his mind whether an attempt to get rid of Wehner, whose position in the parliamentary party was very strong, would have succeeded, although it seems hardly credible that a determined Brandt making full use of the authority of his office would not have won the day. However, Wehner was only articulating more general frustration in the SPD and the country at large, and this general mood found sharper focus with the impact of the oil crisis from October 1973.

Brandt's responses to the crisis did not convey an impression of calm competence; he remained the visionary. It was symptomatic that a writer such a Gunther Grass who had enthusiastically campaigned for Brandt, now admonished him to behave with 'less consciousness of history'.[7] In the same vein much of the liberal press started a positive 'dismantling campaign' of the man whom only shortly before they had raised to superhuman heights. In December when Brandt cele- brated his 60th birthday few articles failed to dwell on the 'weakness of his leadership'. His popularity had plum- meted: the number of those in agreement with his poli- cies dropped from 57 per cent in 1972 to 37–35 per cent in December 1973, the lowest since 1969. His position deteriorated further with the public sector strike and disastrous election results for the SPD in Hamburg in March 1974 where the SPD dropped 11 per cent of its vote. For a while Brandt considered a move to the office of President which would become vacant at the end of Heinemann's term later in 1974, but rejected the idea because, among other reasons, he felt he was indispens- able as party leader. Indeed, it was in the party that he started his fight-back with his '10 April Theses' in which he reimposed party discipline on the left. He was also considering a reshuffle of his cabinet and particularly among his closest staff when the 'Guillaume Affair' broke which was to lead to his resignation.

Guillaume, a former member of the Hitler Youth, had been recruited by the East German Security Services and 'fled' to West Berlin and thence to Frankfurt in 1956 where he earned a living as a freelance photographer and running his mother-in-law's paper shop. He joined the SPD in 1957 and rose by dint of his hard work to become a member of the Frankfurt Town Council. His organiza- tional abilities recommended him for a job in Bonn when after the victory of 1969 the party was short of suitable personnel, although he did not have the academic qualif- ications normally required. He seemed to be a commend- able example of an ordinary man who was overcoming the shortcomings of his background and this required an unconventional approach by his employers. This was also the main reason why he was not more seriously vetted, although there had been some suspicion as to his 'East

German' connections. In 1972 he became Brandt's personal assistant, in charge of all the Chancellor's practical arrangements. Guillaume provided exactly what Brandt needed, the ordering and organizing of details for which the Chancellor had neither time nor inclination. However, by May 1973 enough evidence had emerged to raise serious doubts as to Guillaume's trustworthiness but not enough to secure his arrest. Brandt did not take these allegations very seriously and agreed to keep the matter secret (even from his closest collaborators) and to act as a 'bait' for the German Secret Service. In his insouciance he even went so far as to take Guillaume with him on his annual holiday to Norway in the summer of 1973 where he had access to all communications reaching the Chancellor. It was not until April 1974 that enough material had been collected to make possible an open move against Guillaume who, on his arrest, admitted that he was a citizen of the GDR and an officer of its army. However, subsequent investigations still did not produce sufficient incriminating material, and in order to assess Guillaume's possible access to secret material, Brandt's diaries and members of his entourage came under closer scrutiny. It became clear that Brandt's personal lifestyle and in particular that real or alleged affairs with women journalists would be revealed. Brandt had two choices, either to face exposure in the press or, if this could be avoided, be open to possible pressure from the GDR. However, neither of these options alone were reasons for resignation. There was also the question of where ultimate responsibility for the many and often amazing lapses and inefficiencies lay; but although Brandt accepted the main share, this in itself was again not sufficient reason for resignation. A contributory factor was the lack of support Brandt received from Wehner who felt that the affair was a serious setback for the government and that Brandt might in future be open to blackmail. Wehner's deafening public silence and declarations of loyalty in party circles showed a lack of positive support for Brandt in this crucial situation. After some hesitation Brandt resigned on 6 May. In his speech to the parliamentary party the following day he referred to the feeling of 'continuous pressure' as leader of the government and to his human disappointment over his betrayal by a trusted employee. Both references encapsulated his predicament. For several months he had been exposed to a barrage of criticism which undermined the enthusiasm from which he had gained much of his previous inspiration and which intensified the dreariness of day-to-day government. His disappointment over Guillaume and over all those who had not served him

'We have no idea who pinned that on him.'

adequately was intense; he bemoaned his lack of knowledge of human nature. The fact that Guillaume had spied for the GDR was particularly hurtful. 'What kind of people are they who honour in this way [my] honest attempts to reduce tensions – particularly also between the two German states?' he asked with bitterness in his memoirs. However, Brandt was also at pains to stress the motives for his resignation which went beyond the personal. He resigned 'out of the experiences of the office, out of my ... respect for the unwritten rules of democracy and in order to preserve my personal and political integrity.'[8] Taking all factors into account, however, the impression prevails that Brandt in the 'Guillaume Affair' succumbed to short but even more to longterm factors and that the actual crisis was only the stone which set the avalanche in motion.

Out of Office, 1974–82 5

A recent study of all Chancellors of the Federal Republic reveals the profound impact which the loss of power had on them even if it had been foreseen over a long period or when it came at the end of a long and exhausting career (such as Konrad Adenauer)[1]. For Brandt the change was too abrupt and the doubts about his own conduct in resigning too vivid not to cause a deep personal crisis. According to his memoirs he found some guidance from a leading member of the Protestant Church but although he accepted his fall from power, on the whole, with dignity the next year was perhaps the most difficult of his life. His physical appearance changed: where previously the pressures of office had produced a mask-like face it now appeared puffed up as a result of alcohol consumption and a general increase in weight. However, he soon fell back into a routine of work as party leader and on the international scene too he found that with his great international prestige he could find a new role: he could give impetus to and open new perspectives in the East-West and North-South conflicts by bypassing the existing structures where bureaucracies increasingly immobilized progressive initiatives. The

Presidency of the Socialist International (SI) in 1976 and the Chair of the North-South Commission in 1977 gave him the opportunity to achieve this new role for himself.

CHAIRMAN OF THE GOVERNMENT PARTY

Brandt honoured his pledge to support the new Chancellor loyally and was able to free Schmidt from much of the more mundane party work; Schmidt meanwhile was not held responsible for the shortcomings of the party. However, it soon emerged that their personal differences covered more profound divisions over policy. Schmidt (along with Wehner) was above all committed to a pragmatic course, maintaining the SPD in power, while Brandt, as party leader, was more responsive to its different sections and tried initially to steer a middle course between the party's growing Left and the exigencies of a coalition government; gradually however he veered in favour of the party. This development culminated in the mutual disenchantment between Schmidt and the party and contributed to Schmidt's fall from power in 1982.

The SPD in the early 1970s underwent profound changes as a result of the influx of a large number of young members; of the approximately one million members in 1973 650,000 were 'new' and two thirds were under thirty five. The party's social composition changed accordingly. In 1962 55 per cent of all new members were workers, but by 1972 this number had dropped to 28 per cent, although in society at large workers still made up 44 per cent of the population.[2] The party was thus in danger of losing its traditional base, the working class. On the other hand the number of university and school students had increased substantially and provided the bulk of the party's youth section, the *Jusos.* They brought into the party a hitherto unknown level of preoccupation with theoretical discussion and also an attempt, with their 'march through the institutions', to change the SPD's policies. Their more extreme positions such as that on 'socialism' became increasingly divisive in the party because it threatened the SPD's electoral chances: a survey of 1972 revealed that 53 per cent of those asked would not vote for a government promoting 'socialism'. One year later this figure had risen to 64 per cent.[3] It was therefore not surprising that pragmatic politicians such as Schmidt were the most outspoken critics of the *Jusos*, denouncing them as being blind to reality. Brandt by contrast was in favour not only of opening the party to these new recruits but also of allowing the lively debates within the party which subsequently followed. He emerged more and more as a mediator between the opposing factions. To him 'socialism' as stressed by the left and 'social democracy' as advocated by the right were synonymous. For Brandt socialism was a constant fight for freedom, for justice and for the elimination of the worst inequalities of income and opportunity. However, more conservative elements in the party thought Brandt did not deal forcefully enough with the *Jusos* whose more militant members they believed should be expelled.

In 1976 the SPD won the federal elections again, albeit with a reduced share of the vote (from 45.8 per cent to 42.6 per cent); for the first time in its post-war history it had been deserted by 'Comrade Trend' – the regular increase in its votes at each election. Its partner, the FDP had more or less held its previous vote – a result which strengthened its position at the expense of the SPD. Despite the victory, disenchantment with Chancellor Schmidt grew in the party which was less than enthusiastic about being the Chancellor's 'Election Club'. The parliamentary party was so critical of Schmidt and the many concessions he had made to the smaller partner

The condition of the party.

that in 1977 it threatened to vote against the
government's tax bill. All three leading Social Democrats
exhorted it to keep the coalition alive. Brandt with his
usual historical perspective, compared the situation with
that of 1930 when the SPD had brought down the last
democratic SPD-led cabinet over the comparatively
insignificant issue of contributions to the unemployment
benefit scheme. Brandt identified the lack of *Ruck-
koppelung* (link back) between government and party
as the main cause for discontent. However, Schmidt,
the technocrat, saw in this attempt to involve the
party more directly an impediment to efficient government.

It was ironic that the party should experience its worst
internal divisions at a time when Schmidt was at the

height of his political power. In July 1978 the FRG was the centre of the world economic scene with a summit held in Bonn (the 'Schmidt Summit' because of the German Chancellor's outstanding role). Brezhnev and Queen Elizabeth II had just visited the country which further enhanced the government's standing in the population. This new prestige also helped the SPD to a wave of good election results between 1978 and the spring of 1980. But these successes seemed to widen the gap between the Chancellor and the party and it was only with difficulty that Brandt was able to mediate between them. Thus at the SPD Congress in Berlin (1979) heated debates on the energy and defence issues took place with the Left favouring the renunciation of all nuclear power and the Right fearing for jobs and cheap energy if such a course was followed. Brandt (arguing that in the Third World nuclear energy was indispensable) worked for the compromise by which the party stated its fundamental commitment to coal, although nuclear power should remain as a 'top-up' facility, with a temporary halt in the construction of new nuclear plant. Brandt also helped the acceptance by Congress of NATO's 'Dual Track' policy of which Schmidt had been one of the main architects. (Modernisation of its equipment while at the same time pushing for negotiations. If the latter were unsuccessful the stationing of a new generation of nuclear weapons, Cruise and Pershing, would take place from the autumn of 1983). Although Schmidt thus won the day with Brandt's help the gap between them in fact widened and this was illustrated by the way in which both fought the next election campaign in 1980: Schmidt wanted to be judged on his impressive record but Brandt (and the party) wanted a more long term vision of where the party was going. In the event Schmidt won another convincing personal victory, but while the SPD had increased its vote negligibly to 42.9 per cent the FPD increased its share to 10.6 per cent. The balance in the cabinet thus tilted even further in favour of the liberals which, together with the onset of an economic crisis, led Schmidt to make concessions on policy which the party could no longer accept. Moreover, the SPD parliamentary group had moved further to the left and this made it less amenable to compromise.

Schmidt's third cabinet coincided with the advent to power of President Reagan in the US and a general freeze in East–West relations with Reagan calling the Soviet Union an 'evil empire' and the Soviets invading Afghanistan. In Germany this led to an enormous growth of the Peace Movement which found many sympathizers inside the SPD who feared increasingly that under the NATO 'Dual Track' policy the peace policy of the former Chancellor Brandt seemed in danger. In the autumn of 1981 there were numerous protest demonstrations (against the visit of the US Secretary of State Haig to Berlin in September and against the construction of a new runway at Frankfurt airport in November). There seemed to be a new APO and this together with a deteriorating economic situation (two million unemployed) produced yet another 'German Depression', a widespread and largely irrational feeling of crisis which undermined the government's standing.

In this situation it was critical that Schmidt failed to act more decisively because he was out of action in hospital where a heart pace maker had to be fitted. It seemed an ironic repetition of the situation of 1973: the main political actor, this time Schmidt, was incapacitated, leaving the stage to others, in this case, Brandt. The latter by contrast was emerging from a period of illness and personal crisis (see below) with renewed energies, ready to fight with determination for his objectives both in, and outside Germany. Brandt saw himself more responsible for and more in sympathy with the party than with the difficult task of holding the coalition together. It seemed that his illness and his experience with the North-South Commission had produced a change in his political outlook. He was increasingly abandoning attempts to reach compromises and seemed to accept the party's imminent loss of power. Brandt's change of attitude is well illustrated by his assessment of the fall in 1930 of the last SPD led government before Hitler came to power. Whereas in 1977 he had condemned the SPD's shortsightedness which led the party to give up power too easily, he now held the liberals responsible for the collapse of the last democratic government of Weimar Germany.

The continuing decline of the coalition government was accompanied by the increasingly public differences between Brandt and Schmidt on foreign and defence policy. In foreign affairs these came out clearly after the Soviet invasion of Afghanistan where Schmidt saw in the Soviets' continued stationing of missiles (and the US failure to respond adequately) a dangerous shift in the world balance of power and drew the conclusion that 'détente without a balance of forces is subjection'[4]. Brandt on the other hand, ignoring the military aspect, found that everything possible needed to be done in order to preserve for Europe that measure of détente which had been achieved since 1970, even if this meant distancing himself from the USA. On his return from a visit to Moscow in June 1981 he stressed his conviction that the Soviets were ready to negotiate, but warned of a possible Soviet rearmament. On defence Brandt officially continued to support the NATO position but his views on deployment began to shift. His open sympathy with the Peace Movement was shown in the course of the large peace rally on 10 October 1981 in Bonn, held in protest against the imminent deployment of Cruise and Pershing missiles. Schmidt had appealed to Brandt as party chairman to discourage participation by leading SPD figures in an openly anti-government event – a request which Brandt refused. Although he himself did not take part, other prominent party members did and provided some of the main speakers at the rally.

But it was Brandt's attempts to open the SPD towards the Green and Peace Movements which became most controversial in the autumn of 1981. Brandt felt that as a party reflecting the whole spectrum of society the SPD should integrate this 'no longer ... rebellious but rather resigned youth'[5] in the same way as it had done with sections of the extra-parliamentary opposition in the early 1970s while at the same time not losing the support of its traditional members and voters. For Brandt 'new forms of living together, a new balance between work and leisure, a linking of work and culture' need not be irreconcilable with democratic socialism. He saw in the Peace Movement friends or potential friends. In his view, the SPD's traditional link with the trade unions was not affected by this.

There was considerable opposition to this new course of integration. The SPD had just suffered a dismal defeat in the Berlin elections of May 1981 and although much of this defeat could be blamed on the bad economic situation there were also many who held the confusion in the party and its lack of clear direction responsible. Leading party figures like Richard Lowenthal who for years had collaborated with Brandt singled out Brandt's course of integration as misguided. To Lowenthal the parallel with the 1970s did not apply because '... the mass of peaceful protestors today, do not want to revolutionize society but ... want to drop out of ... [it] and form small islands where they can protect themselves from its dangers'[6]. It was impossible for the SPD, the product of an industrial society, to compromise with drop outs. There was a basic conflict of interests between these different sections of society which needed to be fought out. The conflict became more widely known when Lowenthal issued a shorter six point version of his views and Anneliese Renger (Schumacher's companion and now a leading right winger) circulated them among fifty to sixty chosen addressees with the request for their signature. The most prominent among them was Herbert Wehner, and although Helmut Schmidt was not involved, the campaign was interpreted as an attempt to rebel against Brandt. However, the latter made it clear that a change in direction could only come if the party chose a new chairman. This it was not prepared to do. On the contrary, at its meeting in December 1981 the party's executive fully endorsed Brandt's course of integration.

The party's fortunes did not recover so easily. In March 1982 the SPD suffered a disastrous defeat in Lower Saxony, and it transpired that the party's losses were greatest among the young and skilled labour. The party was beginning to suffer from the 'second best' syndrome with the committed young moving on to the Greens and the solid working class to the CDU. Moreover, it lost 30,000 members in 1981/82. The party's decline continued with another dreadful election result at the beginning of June 1982, this time in Hamburg, Schmidt's home ground.

The Hamburg elections were also a turning point for the FDP which failed to qualify for a seat and was pushed into fourth place by the Green/Alternatives. The smaller coalition partner could see its fortunes sinking if it stayed in a coalition with the ailing SPD. In consequence the party announced that in the forthcoming elections in Hesse in September 1982 it would seek a coalition with the CDU. At the same time the mood in the SPD for an end of the coalition in Bonn also grew. The decision came at the end of August after the trade unions had let it be known that they would fight the government's next round of expenditure cuts.

It was in the long term interests of both Schmidt and the SPD leadership to represent the FDP as responsible for the break-up of the coalition. Brandt, in an article in the SPD Magazine of 26 August, singled out the FDP as a 'political opponent', and at the end of the month the SPD Presidium decided on a new course of confrontation with the FDP: in view of the FDP's obstruction of the budget Schmidt would ask the CDU to arrange a vote of no confidence. This happened in a dramatic session of parliament on 9 September and on the 17th the four FDP ministers were dismissed. On 1 October the vote took place; the government was defeated and after an official change of partner (*die Wende*) the FDP entered the new government under Helmut Kohl. New elections which the SPD had pressed for took place only in March 1983. Brandt seemed to watch these developments with some detachment. By this stage he appeared to have accepted a period of opposition for the party as inevitable if not desirable. Schmidt's and Brandt's contrasting assessment of the events came out clearly in their speeches prior to the vote in the Bundestag on 1 October. Schmidt appealed to his party to maintain a steady line and credibility whereas Brandt laid emphasis on the future where the SPD had to be open to new social forces. Observers felt that Brandt was moving towards a new SPD.

INTERNATIONAL ACTIVITIES

The Socialist International (SI)

The SI is a loose association of originally European socialist parties which come together to exchange views and to coordinate policies. It was founded in 1864 but it has had a mixed history; its most notable defeat came in 1914 when no member had been able to prevent the outbreak of World War I despite the fact that only three weeks earlier they had committed themselves to doing just that by staging a general strike by the workers. In the event patriotism triumphed over international class solidarity. The SI also had a checkered history later and ceased to exist in 1940. It was refounded after World War II as late as 1951 because of the problem of whether to readmit the German SPD. It traditionally had been the most important party in the organization but had been profoundly discredited in the eyes of the other European parties because its members had allowed Hitler into power.

As chairman of the SPD Brandt had been involved in the activities of the SI over several years, and even while he was still Chancellor, in a correspondence with Bruno Kreisky and Olof Palme, the Austrian and Swedish party leaders, he had discussed his ideas of how the SI should develop. It was the task of international social democratic politics to create a world-wide public opinion which could balance the power of international capitalism.

Already in 1974 Brandt emerged as the strongest candidate for the SI Presidency, in succession to the ailing Austrian Pittermann (his name was also mentioned as a possible future General Secretary of the UN), explaining in a number of interviews the role and functions of the organization. He was also active in extending the SPD's international role and in November 1975, for the first time in the party's history, representatives of other Social Democratic Parties were invited to the SPD's Annual Congress. In January 1976 the SPD set up a commission for International Relations at its headquarters with two sub-committees, one for European, the other for Development questions. There were also practical results. In the first instance, the party gave generous aid to the Spanish (PSOE) and Portuguese (PSP) Socialist Parties in their struggle for recognition and power. In post-Franco Spain Brandt was able to provide the party leader Felipe Gonzales with valuable prestige, publicity and financial aid. Brandt also set up a 'Portugal Committee' and as its chairman he was to combat a possible communist takeover in Portugal. He intervened personally with Leonid Brezhnev and Henry Kissinger to prevent their interference in Portugal. German aid through SPD channels contributed to the eventual victory of democratic forces. (In fact the Portuguese Socialist Party, PSP, was founded in exile at Bad Munstereifel in the FRG in 1973; the SPD financed the leader's, Mario Soares, studies in France, and German trade unions trained Portuguese officials).

A first move towards greater involvement in the SI was Brandt's participation in a meeting in May 1976 with the representatives of the socialist parties of three Latin American countries in Caracas, Venezuela. This 'Group of Four' stressed the importance of informal contacts between European and non-European parties. In the SI Brandt emerged more and more as *the* integrative figure who alone seemed to have the ability to unite the feuding wings of the European socialist parties which ranged from the Dutch, with their tenuous membership of NATO, to the German SPD who saw in a strong NATO the precondition for détente in Europe. However, Brandt's German party colleagues were far less enthusiastic, fearing a number of problems for Brandt personally (as a German) and for the government (SI positions contradicting official policies; greater demands on the government's and on SPD's resources). Ultimately, however, it was Chancellor Schmidt himself, perhaps not entirely without self interest, who encouraged Brandt to accept the post.

Brandt was duly elected President of the SI at its Congress in Geneva in December 1976, being proposed by his friend, François Mitterrand of France. From now on Brandt dominated the organization. It was restructured (with 14 Vice-Presidents and a new General Secretary, the Swede Bernt Carlsson, for the administration) in such a way as to leave Brandt free from routine tasks to 'create initiatives for future joint steps'[7] and to give impetus to new beginnings. Brandt also wished to keep the future direction for the SI as vague as possible and therefore prevented the discussion of a precise SI programme at Geneva. A 'Declaration of SI Principles' was adopted only at the Stockholm Congress of 1989 and it contains so many of Brandt's ideas as to be almost his 'Political Testament'.

However, in other ways history seemed to repeat itself for Brandt. The secretary was not as efficient as had been hoped, lacking the clout to overcome Brandt's somewhat indifferent attitude towards organizational matters. This was particularly noticeable when it came to the SI's finances where, despite Carlsson's efforts, the Geneva Congress failed to set up a Finance Committee. (The SI's financial situation remained fraught as Brandt's repeated appeals at subsequent SI events demonstrated.) But although Carlsson's inadequacy was apparent he was not replaced until 1983 (he died in the Lockerbie air disaster of December 1988). Here was another example for Brandt's reluctance to fire personally likeable, but inefficient, subordinates. The SI did not develop into an efficient organization and with its world-wide expansion Brandt's commitments grew out of all proportion. His very popularity (and that of the FRG model of Democratic Socialism and social integration) in the Third World increased the demands on him to such an extent that by October 1982 he seriously considered resignation.

But organizational weaknesses and disagreements on policy paled into insignificance when compared with the visions of the future which Brandt provided and the hitherto unknown enthusiasm with which this filled its members. Brandt signalled a new beginning for the SI: it was to abandon its Euro-centricity and expand into all areas of the globe. It was to launch three offensives: for a secure peace, for new relations between North and South and for Human Rights. Brandt (together with Bruno Kreisky, Olof Palme and Mario Soares) applied all his energy to the new task. He travelled widely, wrote position papers or at least meticulously corrected the drafts of his advisors, gave endless interviews and provided the organization with a new public visibility. Indeed to some observers it was not clear 'whether the SI was a movement or whether it was only Willy Brandt who moved it'[8]. The hectic nature of his lifestyle intensified when at the end of 1978 he also took on the chairmanship of the World Bank-inspired independent North-South Commission (see below), in addition to the burden of the SPD leadership. It was as though with this great burst of activity he tried to recreate some of the tensions and pressures of the lost government office. But he overstretched himself and suffered a severe heart attack in the autumn of 1978.

The years following the Geneva Congress initiated the process of the 'relativization of Europe' in the SI. When in June 1980 the agenda for the next Congress (Madrid) was debated Brandt proposed that 'Europe' need no longer figure as a separate topic for discussion. The SI membership grew rapidly in so many different geographic areas that it seemed increasingly difficult to find a common denominator of shared interests. This was mainly provided by the person of the President.

The hallmark of Brandt's conduct of SI affairs was, in line with his approach to the affairs of the SPD, an attempt to be even-handed. However, despite his efforts the SI's involvement both in Israel and in Latin America proved highly controversial. Thus in Israel he addressed the Congress of the Israeli Labour Party in February 1977; few other Germans could have called, in this forum, for the admission of the rights of the Palestinian Arabs to the realization of their national identity. The SI debated

the Arab/Israel conflict intensively at several meetings
and in 1979 Brandt and Kreisky wrote the 'Vienna Docu-
ment' in which the SI position was reiterated: only
persistent negotiations could produce a settlement of the
problem. In the event it was of course the support of US
President Carter which brought these about at Camp
David from September 1978 and this led to a formal
Peace Treaty in March 1979. But the problem of Palestine
remained intractable; the Israelis could not countenance
a separate Palestinian state. Brandt's efforts thus bore
only limited fruit. However, he and Kreisky continued
their efforts, meeting Yasser Arafat (who saw in Brandt
a 'great moral political force'), and condemning not
only Israel's invasion of Lebanon in 1982 but also
the terrorist actions against Israeli diplomats, as well
as 'state terrorism'. The whole question became so
controversial within the SI that a meeting in Israel
planned for June 1981 was cancelled. Brandt who had
already acquired a reputation of 'moving left' calmed the
waters with difficulty (he was to perform a similar
balancing act during the debates on the Falklands War
when European and Latin American members dramatically opposed each other, threatening a public condemnation of the UK).

The SI's involvement and Brandt's position became
particularly controversial in Nicaragua where in July 1979
the Somoza dictatorship was overthrown by the Marxist-
dominated Frente Sandinista de Liberacion. The new
government established links with Cuba and the Soviet
Union and this brought it into conflict with the USA. As
the Americans consider Central America to be their
sphere of influence they were, notably under President
Reagan, prepared to fight for it in the form of aid to the
anti-Sandinista Contras. This stiffened the determination
of the other side, and SI support for it. Observers noted a
tougher SI style: whereas as late as 1976 the SI (and particularly its president) had tried to convince the USA,

there was now a note of confrontation. Although Brandt denied this there was a growing anti-American mood not only among Latin American members but also among the young, notably in Europe. The position of the moderates and also Brandt's own became more difficult. He continued to stress that it was not the aim of the SI to take sides (although his own sympathies were with the 'admirable struggle of the Nicaraguan people'), but he was increasingly caught between all fronts as controversies broke out among European SI members some of whom believed Brandt to be too sympathetic to Nicaragua. Moreover, his standing with the USA was by now very low. Jeanne Kirkpatrick had become the American representative at the UN and for her and President Reagan (whose ear she had) Latin America was of vital importance to the interests of the USA: the SI's activities there were 'wholly unacceptable'. Brandt became *persona-non grata* with Reagan to such an extent that when Reagan visited the Federal Republic in May 1985 to commemorate the end of the war he refused to receive Brandt.

Brandt focused increasingly on the third main area of SI activities, détente/disarmament which became more important for him because here Europeans (and he personally) could make a contribution and because it was closely connected to his successful *Ostpolitik*. He saw in progress here the key to many of the world's most pressing problems; disarmament could make available the means to help the world's poorest. (See below.)

The 'Securing of Peace' (*Friedenssicherung*) in Europe had of course been the basis of Brandt's *Ostpolitik* and preoccupation with the subject did not cease with his job as Chancellor. He took a passionate interest in the Helsinki Conference (1975) with its long term objective of détente and commitment of the Eastern Bloc to Human Rights. He believed it represented a great step forward for Europe. Moreover, in numerous interviews and in the SI he worked against the formal linkage of the Eastern Bloc's record on Human Rights with the process of détente. In fact, Brandt suspected, the opponents of détente used the East's poor Human Rights record to jeopardize détente. The SI set up a special Working Group for Disarmament under the Fin Kalevi Sorsa which in April 1978 held a first conference in Helsinki. It was attended by high ranking Soviet and American representatives. At this time the Soviets tried to mobilize Brandt personally for a new international disarmament initiative in the form of an independent commission along the lines of the North-South Commission. However, international developments soon moved away from this kind of enthusiasm for détente, although Brandt continued to cultivate his good connections with the USSR. Brandt remained realistic as to the impact the SI could achieve: although 'the work of the SI met everywhere with lively interest', it was not certain whether a new twist of the armament screw could be avoided. Indeed, in the autumn of 1983 a new generation of rockets (Pershing and Cruise) was deployed in the FRG and in other European countries.

THE NORTH-SOUTH COMMISSION

In March 1977 Brandt was approached by the President of the World Bank, Robert McNamara, offering him the chair of a planned independent North-South Commission. Although interested in principle Brandt hesitated over his decision. Other, similar commissions (such as that headed by the Canadian ex-Prime Minister Lester Pearson in 1969) had been set up whose reports had made little lasting impact. Moreover, in 1977 another North-South conference, the Conference on International Economic Cooperation, was meeting in Paris where the developing countries, organized in the 'Group 77', had been negotiating in vain for better trade conditions with the industrial states. These negotiations had come to nothing and the planned Brandt Commission was regarded by this group with particular suspicion as an attempt by the rich nations to play for time in order to alleviate the strong international pressures exercised after the oil crisis. Brandt nevertheless accepted McNamara's offer because he was given strong encouragement by many governments, organizations and individuals. After a careful analysis of previous endeavours in this area he came to the conclusion that an 'additional attempt by an independent group could be helpful ... with suggestions improving the general atmosphere, pointing out certain perspectives and common interests and thus also influencing public opinion.' This had been the approach of his successful *Ostpolitik* which gave him 'the additional impetus'[9]. Brandt, who up to this time had not shown strong interest in development questions, now began to consider the tackling of the North-South divide as *the* social question to be solved during the remainder of the century. He compared the relations between North and South to the class struggle of the past with the rich countries in the position of the employers and the poor in that of the industrial workers.

To win support for the venture it was essential to demonstrate the Commission's independence; it was therefore not financed by the World Bank but relied on donations and would submit its final report with recommendations to the UN which would remain responsible for future formal negotiations. On this basis Brandt was quickly able to win the support of the 'threshold' countries i.e. those who were about to industrialize. Brandt managed to dispel the reservations of the poorest countries who were most reluctant to put their faith in yet another western-inspired initiative by a series of personal visits to several Third World countries. Even where enthusiasm for the venture remained muted, the person of the chairman was explicitly exempted from the criticism.

Support in the 'first world' was also not automatically forthcoming. Thus Brandt's own West German government was ambiguous. Chancellor Schmidt found Third World criticism of the rich nations' modest development aid (*kapitalistische Ausbeuter*) unacceptable; the federal government refused to make a financial contribution to the Commission's work; instead this came from the party affiliated foundations. Fortunately for the venture, other governments, notably the Dutch, were more forthcoming. However, finance remained a permanent problem.

Meanwhile Brandt proceeded with the selection of the members of the Commission. This was not easy as the criteria – independent personalities of international standing and their availability – were difficult to match. Eventually a list of seventeen members emerged with ten from the 'Third World' which thus had a majority, another indication of Brandt's endeavours to calm existing suspicions. The Commission was finally convened for the first time at Schloss Gymnich near Bonn in December 1977. It submitted its final report at the beginning of 1980. In the course of the two years of its deliberations it met ten times in nine countries; a large number of experts were heard (including those of the Eastern Bloc which previously had refused to cooperate claiming that poverty in the Third World was a result of western colonialism and hence not their problem), and several visits into areas of special needs for 'on the spot' investigations were undertaken. Brandt's personal involvement was considerable; by September 1978 he had spoken to many statesmen from the Third World as well as to 'nearly all heads of government in the Western and Communist states'.

There was a small secretariat in Geneva and although a development economist took general notes at the Commission's deliberations no detailed minutes nor tape recordings were made. Only summaries in French and English were produced; the anonymity of the proceedings ensured unhindered, free discussions and a 'pleasant working atmosphere'.

Work on the Commission alerted Brandt more and more to the urgent needs of the Third World. Thus while in an interim report in 1978 he referred to the 'mutuality of interests' between the rich and the poor, a new urgency came into Brandt's pronouncements by the summer of 1979 with the realization of the mass starvation and the chronic shortage of energy in the Third World.

As the work of the Commission neared completion Brandt's comments about the future of the poorest nations became more pessimistic. At the press conference on 17 December 1979 after its last meeting at Leeds Castle (England) he outlined the main findings of the Commission. Far-reaching measures were urgently needed to prevent a catastrophe; he reserved his most emotive language ('deeply shocking', 'shameful') to describe the fate of the world's poorest. Three fundamental changes were required not only to secure their survival but to prevent major confrontations. These were: long-term structural reforms of the world economy, a change in the power structures of the world which would lead to a 'better functioning and more effective world community' and a World Development Fund, a world-wide institution with broadly based participation. To alleviate the threat of a world economic crisis the Commission proposed an emergency programme; a 'parcel' of measures was to bring benefits to all sides: to the industrial states, the oil producers, the 'threshold' and the very poorest countries; there were to be increased, broadly based transfers of resources to the

Third World, an agreement to secure energy supplies and savings, an effective world food programme together with basic reforms in some critical areas such as that of the currency system and the financing of development programmes. These demands were of course justified by the desperate situation in parts of the Third World and reflect the views of the Commission as a whole. Nevertheless, they implied major, not to say revolutionary changes on a vast scale which, with the world political scene shifting, had little chance of realization.

The Brandt Report *North-South: A Programme for Survival*, was published in more than twenty languages. But its publication took place against the background of the revolution in Iran and the Soviet invasion of Afghanistan which led to a dramatic deterioration in the relations among the superpowers. Moreover, Reagan was committed to replacing pluralism in international relations with bi-partite arrangements. For the Third World he advocated 'greater self-reliance', a euphemism the true meaning of which became clear when the US actually cut its contributions to the UN sponsored International Development Agency. In this climate the report had less lasting impact than Brandt had hoped for. It was raised at the Venice summit of June 1980 which welcomed it and promised to look carefully at its recommendations. 'However, the matter rested there,'[10] Brandt concluded ruefully. Parliaments of various countries and the parliament of the European Community debated the report; working parties were set up and several governments redefined their guidelines in the light of the Brandt Report's recommendations. 'However, no notice was taken of our proposals for fundamental reform'. The IMF and the World Bank adopted several of the report's suggestions but this came rather late. On the other hand the report captured the imagination of thousands of individuals and groups. In London 10,000 people came to

Parliament to take part in a 'lobby on Brandt'. There were mass meetings in Berlin and The Hague at which action on the basis of 'Brandt' was demanded. In October 1981 an international summit which the report had advocated took place at Cancun (Mexico). However, the invitation to only twenty two nations created ill feelings among those not invited and President Reagan's attendance while the Soviets stayed away deprived it of much of its impetus. Moreover, both the Austrian Chancellor Kreisky and the West German Chancellor Helmut Schmidt were absent due to illness. No concrete decisions were taken due to 'the delaying tactics of the US and its hard-core allies'.

Two main criticisms were levelled at the Brandt Commission: that it had not demanded more efforts from the developing nations themselves and that its development concept was wrong, even though the report had given an apt description of the conditions in the Third World. However, according to Brandt it was not the situation inside individual developing countries which had been the focus of the Commission's attention but 'the relations between the industrial and developing countries, the existing world economic order and the possibilities of improving it.' On the other hand no definition of 'development' had been attempted because 'our concern was not with fine points of theory but with the fact that there is hunger in the world, that too many children die, that many millions live in unimaginable poverty. In short, we believed that something urgently needed to be done to improve the situation ...'[11] Even in this wider sense Brandt's position was questioned by experienced development workers as the Commission's recommendations always seemed to address themselves to governments rather than the people on the ground. There was evidence that projects financed with development money left people poorer than before; that food imports led to the reduction of food grown internally. Brandt naturally rejected these strictures and revealed himself as the politician he had always remained. From the outset the Commission was to be a *political* one, concerned with moving matters at the highest level by changing perspectives and influencing public opinion, although in view of this surprisingly little thought was given to the proper 'selling' of the report's main ideas. The problems involved were global, requiring a united response which in the overall political and economic climate of the 1980s was not forthcoming. This was responsible for the lack of long term impact of the Brandt Report.

However, despite this comparative failure Brandt never abandoned the issue. There were two directions in which work continued. Firstly, a direct extension of the Brandt Committee's activities for which Brandt mobilized the SI and secondly, based on the connection between 'development and disarmament', a growing emphasis on pressure for détente. (See Chapter 6.)

At the beginning of 1983 a second report of the North-South Commission was published as *Common Crisis* and later that year the SI Congress in Madrid took place under the motto 'The World in Crisis: The Socialist Response'. This Congress set up an SI Committee on Economic Policy, chaired by the former Prime Minister of Jamaica Michael Manley, which in September 1985 published its findings as *Global Challenge* for which Manley and Brandt wrote a joint introduction. In it the authors saw the current international crisis as worse than that of the 1930s. There was global deflation and crippling debts for which the IMF was singled out for blame. Against the 'trickling down' effect of monetarism international reflation was advocated as well as a strategy for development and disarmament. 'We need a new model of development, based on the recovery of growth through redistribution, rather than redistribution from growth.' But this redistribution would only be possible if accompanied by a fundamental restructuring of the ownership and traditional patterns of resource allocation, as advocated in the 1970s as the New International Economic Order (NIEO). The report itself was much more openly critical of the US (and of several other members of the Group of Ten) and called for 'a new role for Europe' which should include a clear alignment with the Third World.

In reality the wealthier European states were not much more positive in their attitudes towards the south than the US although the latter's intransigence served as a perfect cover. This emerged clearly in the failed attempt to increase the funds of the UN's International Development Agency (IDA) in 1984. Its replenishment up to $12 billion failed owing to US obstruction which gave the German Chancellor Helmut Kohl a perfect excuse not to be more generous. No solution was found at the Economic Summit in London (6–9 June 1984) either, which Brandt found 'extremely disappointing'. To him there was now little prospect for dealing with the crucial issues affecting the Third World. In, for him, uncharacteristically sharp language he condemned the whole rigmarole of summitry: 'Summits of this form and with so little concrete results are not only useless, they are actually harmful as they add to the uncertainty already existing in the international economy ... We should stop this summit show. Instead we need an emergency meeting on IDA and the international debt crisis.'[12] Eventually the World Bank approved the figure of $9 billion mainly because of last minute help from Kuwait who acknowledged Brandt's contribution in putting pressure on all concerned.

His work with the North-South Commission, the first hand knowledge of abysmal poverty and human suffering in the world, as well as that of the selfish indifference of the 'other side' were for Brandt another formative experience which affected his general political outlook. From now on almost every public speech referred to the plight of the Third World. It was therefore perhaps not surprising that he found some of the minutiae of the SPD and of German politics increasingly tedious.

The Elder Statesman, 1982-90

6

CHAIRMAN OF THE SPD IN OPPOSITION (1982-7)

Although the immediate response to Schmidt's overthrow was an emotional surge of support for the SPD with good election results in Hesse and in Hamburg, once Schmidt was replaced by Hans Jochen Vogel as Chancellor candidate the party's chances of winning the forthcoming federal elections of March 1983 were remote. The SPD lost the 'Schmidt-Faktor' which was estimated at 5 per cent of the votes. The new candidate was hardworking but lacked charisma (Brandt characterized him as 'the one with the see-through folders'). The result of 38.2 per cent for the SPD was therefore disappointing but hardly surprising. This was followed by dramatic changes for the party: immediately after the election Herbert Wehner announced his resignation from politics due to illness, but also because his main objective, to install and keep the SPD in power, had come to such obvious grief. With Schmidt also soon to retire from politics (he announced his resignation from the *Bundestag* after the Cologne Annual Congress of November 1983) Brandt was the lone political survivor of the *troika*. It was no mean achievement. After the years in the political wilderness following his resignation as Chancellor he had carved out a new role for himself: as President of the Socialist International and Chairman of the North-South Commission he had maintained his undisputed international stature. He had also come through another traumatic personal crisis with a heart attack in the autumn of 1978 which, after it had remained undetected for several weeks, was more difficult to overcome. Moreover, while convalescing in the south of France he was helped with liaison with SPD headquarters by an attractive party worker, Brigitte Seebacher, and this led to the ending of Brandt's second marriage. He had been married to Rut for over thirty years; she had been popular in the party and respected by the population at large for her unstinting support of Brandt during the dramatic days of 1972 and, even more, after his resignation in 1974. Brandt therefore initially had to accept a drop in his popularity. However, his new marriage (1983) has had a rejuvenating effect which, together with his almost total abstention from alcohol and cigarettes gave him energy for a new beginning.

He was now undisputed leader of the party, and with definite ideas for its future. Partly as the result of the personal 'learning process' which we have noted, partly because of inner party pressure he saw the need for a modernization of the SPD. While he still adhered to the old *Volkspartei* of the Godesberg Programme he believed that the party should be brought into line with the new majorities of those who tried to reconcile economy and ecology, environmental and peace concerns and develop new more humane forms of living in a multi-cultural society. These concepts also implied a fundamental change on defence thinking and a rejection of nuclear energy. It was the attempt to disguise these changes for the sake of party unity which had led the party to appear with an unclear public message. However, Brandt and his supporters on the left of the party (from now on in a

Marble, stone, and iron break ...

majority at annual Party Congresses) believed that in the long run the public would come to endorse their views. Future majorities were to be found, in Brandt's words, 'to the left of the CDU': the majority of Germany's youth was reckoned to be 'left'.

This shift to the left was reflected in the party's renewed preoccupation with a new programme. While Brandt in the early 1970s had disparaged this as an 'inner-party playground'[1] for the Jusos he now became the chairman (up to 1987) of the relevant committee, although his main contribution seems to have been not so much an input of original ideas but once again to create an environment in which the articulation of different points of view could take place. (The new programme was finally adopted in December 1989). Partly as a result of this so many new concepts were

131

generated that at its meeting in Irsee (Bavaria) in 1986 the commission presented over forty propositions (the 'Irsee Programme'). Consequently, Brandt called a temporary halt to the proceedings: 1986 was pre-election year and all energies had to focus on this task. More important were the party's internal divisions which left it without a clear stance notably on economic policy and this reinforced the damaging public impression of disunity and lack of realism.

In terms of policy the realization of Brandt's ideas meant for the SPD a swing to the left and the abandoning of the (at times tenuous) general West German consensus on defence and social policy which had existed in the country since the Godesberg Programme. On the defence issue this became clear when in October 1983 Brandt took part in a vast peace demonstration in Bonn, the climax of a week of protest actions organized by the Peace Movement, and denounced the deployment of NATO missiles which was to take place in December after the US-Soviet negotiations had failed. But to some extent he only voiced an opinion widespread in the SPD as a whole so that at its annual congress in Cologne in November 1983 they voted decisively against deployment (383:14 with 3 abstentions). Schmidt had only won thirteen members to support his position and this led him to resign from the *Bundestag*. This stance however did not endear the SPD to the Peace Movement because for the latter the SPD remained suspect, as the party did not waver in its commitment to NATO and approved of the revival of the West European Union with its 'Europeanization' of defence. Brandt in a well publicized interview had also laid stress on an increase of conventional arms and this could not satisfy the more far reaching aspirations of the Peace Movement.

The social policy issue centred on the shortening of the working week with full pay, and went to the heart of the market economy as it might have led to a loss in competitiveness of German industry and hence to the loss of jobs (according to the right), or to a more equitable distribution of the benefits of a capitalist economy (the view of the left of the party). In February 1984 Brandt came out in support of the metal and print trade unions' claim for a thirty-five hour week on full pay, in order to bridge the gulf which had opened up between unions and the SPD. However, the CDU backed the employers and this direct involvement by the big parties in an industrial conflict signalled the end of the previously prevailing party political neutrality in this area. Brandt himself recognized that this interlocking (*Schulterschluss*) with the unions was not unproblematical for the SPD because other social democratic trade union leaders had agreed pay settlements without a reduction in working hours. Moreover, only 61 per cent of all local branches were prepared to support the party leadership on this issue.

A further reason for Brandt's position on this question was that the thirty-five hour week could be presented to the public as a 'greening' of the SPD. However, despite Brandt's efforts to integrate environmentalists into the SPD, Green activists distrusted the tactics of the SPD on the nuclear question and recalled Brandt's record when he as Chancellor had moved against alternative forces in the FRG with his decree against radicals. To the public at large the SPD remained first and foremost an industrial party where commitment to 'green' issues such as the rejection of nuclear power coexisted uneasily with trade union demands to preserve nuclear power for the sake of jobs. It was another prime example for 'on the one hand – but on the other': the party accepted and rejected 'growth' (this time through nuclear energy) simultaneously. Brandt's own commitment on these issues had developed only gradually over the years from his reference to the 'blue sky over the Ruhr' of 1961 (owing much to American influences on his election campaign then) to the inclusion of 'green' issues in the reform programme of 1969 (giving them a low priority among more pressing concerns), to the early 80s when he had still seen nuclear power as indispensable. By August 1986 however he took a leading part in an Anti-Nuclear Rock Festival on the Loreley outside Bonn, to demonstrate the 'readiness of politicians to learn' although the impact on the general public seemed ambiguous. It revealed in him yet again an endearing human quality of openness to new ideas – which was so appreciated by the young – but it also smacked of political opportunism or even of eccentricity.

Moreover, Brandt's efforts were undermined by a general greening of German politics and by a growing radicalization of the Green Movement itself. Many state governments including those CDU controlled ones such as Bavaria and Baden-Württemberg endorsed green policies, whereas the SPD which actually went into a coalition with the Green party in Hesse in December 1985, did not benefit from this move as the coalition suddenly collapsed on 9 February 1987. This reflected the fact that after Chernobyl (April 1986) the Greens had become more radical with their 'fundamentalist' wing in the ascendancy which emerged at their Party Congress in 16–19 May 1986 and in violent demonstrations in June/ July 1986 at Wackersdorf and Brockdorf. These showed the Greens as dangerously extremist and therefore no partner for a serious party like the SPD. A red/green coalition in Bonn became thus more difficult. In the long run the disaster at Chernobyl in April 1986 did not work to the SPD's advantage because it spurred the government into action, stressing mainly the necessity of improved safety, rather than rejecting nuclear power altogether (with all the social and economic implications this entailed.)

In the light of these developments Brandt's floating of the idea of a new coalition with the CDU appears as a somewhat unreal attempt to keep the SPD in the limelight of publicity. This coalition was to be based on *nationale Verantwortung* (national responsibility) for the

(Greens)   (Greens)

areas of unemployment, environment, pension reform, Europe and a second round of *Ostpolitik*. It was an opportunistic attempt to exploit the temporary discomfort of the CDU and of Chancellor Kohl in particular, who was deeply implicated in the 'Flick Affair' (exact records of payments to political parties had been discovered in the papers of Flick's manager). In the autumn of 1985 Kohl emerged as the least popular Chancellor for over two decades; against this the SPD's position looked far better with election victories in two recent state elections. However, there was so little common ground between the two big parties that Brandt's moves achieved little in re-establishing the SPD as a serious contender for power.

The year 1986 was not a good year for either the SPD or Brandt personally. Personal tensions in the party leadership surfaced once again, and certain fundamental mistakes were made which ultimately led to Brandt's resignation. In the first instance the party had to choose a new candidate for Chancellor as the elections in

Willy, our contortionist.

January 1987 approached and the recent election victory of the SPD in North-Rhine-Westphalia determined the choice of Johannes Rau, the party leader there. He was initially fully endorsed by Brandt but relations between the two men soon deteriorated. This was partly due to the candidate himself who was reluctant to take on the challenge and made his acceptance dependent on his endorsement by the Party Congress in Nuremberg, in August 1986. He was also unwilling to formulate his own clear political line. However, what eventually emerged was designed to irritate Brandt: a firm commitment not to form a coalition with the Greens. This recipe had been successful in Rau's state but to Brandt such a categorical rejection of the Greens might cause problems in other states. Moreover, Rau was also firmly in favour of NATO and the US and critical of the Brandt/Bahr initiatives on Working Parties with the SED (see below) and the leadership's general lack of orientation in security policy. He made no bones about his intention of wanting to win back the political middle ground which he needed in order to reach his aim: outright victory for the SPD alone which would solve the awkward problem of having to find a coalition partner. These views were of course akin to those of the party's Schmidtite faction which increasingly warmed to the candidate and although Rau declared his intention of wanting to be the candidate of the whole party he was increasingly seen as that of the right. Only the candidate's indecisive personality (his nickname was 'Bruder Johannes', Brother John) prevented him from being built up as an open challenger to the chairman. Brandt's enthusiasm for Rau accordingly cooled noticeably and this became public knowledge. When Brandt for example praised the effective conduct of the CDU's pre-election campaign, he implied that his own party was at fault. He also openly distanced himself from Rau with a statement to the press while on holiday in the south of France, that 43 per cent for the SPD was 'quite a good result'. It was this in itself innocuous remark which indirectly contributed to Brandt's fall.

The statement certainly corresponded to the actual overall standing of the SPD in popular opinion where it had fallen from 45 per cent in the autumn of 1985 to 35–38 per cent in the summer of 1986[2] and Rau's objective of all out victory looked more and more unrealistic. However, for Brandt to acknowledge this openly seemed another disavowal of the SPD's official candidate. Furthermore, in the autumn of 1986 Brandt added to the confusion in the party (and its public image of divisiveness) by announcing his intention of resigning the party leadership in 1988. Brandt has since admitted that this was an error of judgement on his part as it opened the door to speculations about his successor at a time when all the party's energies should have focused on the election campaign. There was also the resounding scandal and collapse in September 1986 of the SPD Housing Association, *Neue Heimat*, which tainted the party with corruption and inefficiency.

Tensions between Brandt and Rau grew to such a pitch that in November 1986 the spokesman for the SPD Executive Committee resigned: at the same time he gave up the post of Rau's campaign manager so as not to come into a conflict of loyalties between Brandt and Rau. The search was now on for a new spokesman; it was decided that it should be a woman to project the party's endeavour to give women a higher profile. Brandt proposed the highly intelligent and internationally educated daughter of old friends, Margarita Matheopoulos. As the name indicates her parents were Greek although she was born in Germany but she was neither a member of the SPD (in fact she turned out to be a CDU sympathizer) nor particularly experienced in the handling of the media. However, she was good looking with an easy manner and to Brandt she seemed ideally suited to make a statement about the party's image of modern world-openness. The choice turned out to be a serious error of judgement which might appeal to intellectuals but ignored the 'soul of the party'. In the words of one official: 'our party represents the the "little man" and he does not think like that'[3]. Brandt was now blamed for all the ills which had befallen the party in the previous years and notably for the most recent defeat in the January 1987 federal elections where the SPD had polled only 37 per cent (although the CDU's vote was also much reduced with 44.3 per cent, the winners being the FDP with 9.1 per cent and the Greens with 8.3 per cent).

Brandt resigned as party leader on 23 March 1987 to an enormous public stir both inside and outside the Federal Republic. As in 1974 when he resigned as Chancellor foreign observers failed to understand how a man of Brandt's stature could resign for such an insignificant reason. However, the deeper cause of Brandt's action seems to lie in the realization, as in 1974, that the job had outgrown his capacities. His strategy for rejuvenating the SPD was succeeding but at a price and a speedy resumption of power was not in sight. Although in the SPD it was claimed that a 'sigh of relief' was passing through the party and that the period of squabbles and uncertainties was over, Brandt's going was also seen as a great loss. As a leading functionary put it: 'Because of the old man, the SPD was something special in the world. Now we shall be quite an ordinary socialist party in Europe.'[4]

THE INTERNATIONAL SCENE

The affairs of the SPD were always only one of several fields of interest for Brandt and his international activities at times seemed to dwarf the significance of internal party squabbles (hence the impression of remoteness he sometimes projected), at others they shed light on his moves inside the party and in German politics generally. Thus his relations with Schmidt were soured further by the latter's lukewarm suport for the North-South Commission's report. The disappointing reception of the report by the US government as well as Brandt's clashes with the US in his capacity of President of the SI over Latin America contributed to his increasingly critical stance towards the Reagan administration. Brandt's shift on defence issues later in 1983 when he voted with the party's majority against the stationing of Pershing and Cruise followed on logically. He regretted that for too long he had been silent about his real views concerning the US involvement in Vietnam which he (wrongly) thought had always been negative. For Brandt the result of the 1987 election would bring a decision on whether the FRG under a conservative government would join those states which considered that 'might was right' as the most important principle in North-South relations and

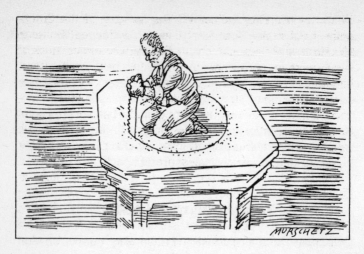

Do It Yourself

which treated national freedom movements as terrorists.

Despite the seeming setbacks to *Ostpolitik* in the new
Cold War climate (following the invasion of Afghanistan,
the declaration of martial law in Poland, the continued
stationing of Soviet SS20s in Eastern Europe and the US
SDI project) and to the North-South Commission Report
at a time of economic recession and monetarism, Brandt
continued to pursue disarmament and the Third World.
He grew increasingly aware that a solution to many
problems in the Third World was more likely if the
expenditure on arms around the globe could be limited
and this became the main focus for the future of the
North-South Commission's work. Although formally
dissolved after its report had been submitted individual
members continued to meet on an ad hoc basis. In
January 1984 they met together with the Independent
Commission for International Security and Disarmament
(Olof Palme, its chairman, was also a member of the
Brandt Commission) in Rome where they were received

by the Pope. They welcomed the opening of the Stock-holm Conference for Safety and Confidence Building Measures and Disarmament in Europe, the endeavours of some leading politicians to push for new multi-lateral initiatives and the continuation of the Geneva Conference on Disarmament. They referred to the appalling imbalance between military spending and that for peaceful (and development) purposes: only 0.1 per cent of the world's military budget of 1984 would triple the UN's funds for peace securing measures.

For Brandt the arms reduction process had to begin in Europe where the two military camps were confronting each other. Already in September 1983 he had presented a Four Point proposal to a special Hearing of the US Congress which endorsed the demands of the US and European Peace Movements, demanding both the renunciation by the US of the stationing of Cruise and Pershing missiles and a considerable reduction of SS20s which were facing Europe. The various arms reduction negotiations should be coordinated and the arsenal of nuclear arms in both countries should be reduced. On 22 November 1983, a month after his participation in the Bonn Peace rally, he placed an advertisement in the *Frankfurter Zeitung*: '"Before it is too late" International Appeal for the Support of Willy Brandt's Four Point Plan for Détente. Personalities from inside and outside the FRG appeal to Washington and Moscow.' In the spring of 1985 Brandt came out in support of the Four-Continent initiative for peace and disarmament by the governments of Sweden, India, Greece, Mexico and Argentina who thus signalled their determination not to leave this vital matter to the superpowers alone. The SI continued its activities in the field and in October 1985 held a Conference for Problems of Peace and Security in Vienna. The Soviet Union, the USA and China were represented.

At the Vienna meeting Brandt made the opening speech and referred specifically to the constructive

Soviet proposal to reduce nuclear arms; indeed in the new Soviet President Gorbachev, Brandt had found a politician not unlike himself: a man who was open to new ideas, eager to learn and prepared to exchange views in open debate; who realized that the World's current problems required a global approach; with the vision of a freer, fairer society and the determination to act upon this vision once the opportunity arose. Gorbachev, on the other hand, acknowledged the truly invaluable experience of the early 1970s in which the good political, legal and moral-psychological bases for cooperation between states of both systems was created. Moreover, it seems that Brandt's later ideas also found a direct echo in Gorbachev's. Brandt was the first western politician whom Gorbachev received on coming to power. He welcomed Brandt by endorsing his views on the Third World with which he was 'well familiar'. For both men the time seemed to be approaching when a new economic order tackling the problem of the indebtedness of the Third World would become the object of comprehensive international discussions. In his book *Perestroika* (1987) Gorbachev still refers explicitly to the Report of the North-South Commission. Several of Gorbachev's later proposals were akin to those put forward by Brandt in previous years such as 'disarmament for development' or the necessity of 'new thinking': when approaching the problems of the nuclear/cosmic age which confronted mankind with the issue of its survival there was a joint task – to save human civilization from a nuclear catastrophe. Another of Gorbachev's concepts, 'mutual interest' or 'mutual dependence', seemed equally close to Brandt's ideas when he suggested that the Soviet Union's foreign policy never separated Soviet security needs from those of others. Brandt himself had based his *Ostpolitik* precisely on this pragmatism.

There was not only proximity in the ideas but also in the politics of the two men. Even before the advent of

Gorbachev to power one of the hallmarks of *Ostpolitik* had been that Brandt accepted the legitimate interests of the Eastern bloc countries and this circumspection also characterized his dealing with the Soviet Union later. Thus, when martial law was imposed in Poland in 1980 his response was muted (a stance which was heavily criticized in the SI) in recognition of the delicate situation there. Brandt also travelled to China only in 1984, making it clear that no 'encirclement' of the Soviet Union was intended. On the other hand he had been frank about his views in letters to Leonid Brezhnev and Juri Andropov. To Gorbachev he recommended a spectacular gesture, such as the unilateral nuclear test ban by the Soviet Union, as a beginning of a process which might lead to a reduction in armaments which ordinary people everywhere desired. In following this approach Gorbachev would take up the policy that had been J.F. Kennedy's in 1963, although at that time a more far reaching agreement had not come about because of the lack of effective means of verification. Although Gorbachev initially rejected the idea (which was also proposed by others) – insisting on the, by now, traditional Soviet position of 'mutuality' with the US – he did actually announce it on 6 August 1985, the 40th anniversary of the dropping of the first atomic bomb by the Americans – and scored the first major publicity success in the battle for western public opinion. This first test ban led to UN Resolution L 49, calling for a Limited Test Ban Treaty (LTBT) which was initiated by the Four-Continent-Group and supported by the group 'Parliamentarians for World Order', by distinguished members of former US administrations and by Brandt who, after the passing of the resolution in December 1985, appealed to both superpowers to end all test explosions from the beginning of 1986. But despite intense international and US pressure on the White House and an offer by Gorbachev of third party verification, Reagan exploded another atomic bomb on

23 March 1986. However, a process had got underway in which Gorbachev, who continued his unilateral test stop, increasingly gained the initiative which culminated in the near-agreement on far reaching disarmament at the summit at Reykjavik in October 1986 and the signing of the INF Treaty of December 1987.

While Brandt's (and others') attempts to influence the superpowers seemed to be bearing fruit in that they were moving closer to armament limitations, he remained acutely aware of Europe's dependence on these decisions and it seemed more important than ever for the Europeans themselves to develop new initiatives. European and particularly German interests did not always coincide with those of the superpowers; indeed the very strength of the Peace Movement in both Germanies indicated the growing distrust and fear of many of the ever increasing weight of military hardware in their countries. On this basis, and in the attempt to limit damage to the environment, Brandt sought closer contacts with East European countries. From the early 1980s the SPD established closer links with the SED in the GDR. In October 1986 joint principles for a 300 km wide nuclear free corridor either side of the Iron Curtain comprising the FRG in the west and the GDR and Czechoslovakia in the east were published which echoed the proposals made by the Palme Commission earlier. This proposal also aimed at a reduction in conventional arms which would lead to a reduction in the 'structural ability to attack' ('*verminderte strukturelle Angriffsfahigkeit*') which in the eyes of Brandt and the SPD was the best guarantee for the avoidance of a future armed conflict in Europe.

Brandt held talks about the environment with Czechoslovakia (November 1985); contacts between the SPD parliamentary party and its counterpart in Prague were established. As in the SPD there were discussions in Prague on 'Work and Environment' but both initiatives suffered from impediments outside Brandt's control:

Moscow distrusted the all-German *rapprochement* and forced the East German leader Honecker to cancel his visit to the FRG (he came only in September 1987); economic considerations prevented much action on the environment in Czechoslovakia. On the contrary, the visit by an SPD delegation which wished to follow up Brandt's contacts in November 1985 was cancelled by the Czechs. Moreover, a humanitarian bargain which Brandt had struck with President Husak on behalf of the son of the Czech President, Jiri Hajek, during the 'Prague Spring' of 1968, was also not honoured by the Czech authorities.

It seemed thus that Brandt's foreign policy initiatives in Eastern Europe faltered on the overall immobility of the eastern bloc. For this reason the activities were not uncontroversial in – and outside the SPD. During the 1987 election campaign for example SPD candidate Rau vetoed a new *Ostpolitik* initiative, as advocated by Brandt and the SPD security expert Bahr. Conservatives labelled it *Nebenaussenpolitik* (Parellel Foreign Policy). Certainly when the great thaw occurred in the eastern bloc the SPD's contacts with the now discredited former rulers and the party's comparative neglect of opposition circles temporarily left it in some disarray. This had to be placed against the fact that continued efforts had been made to maintain contacts and improve the situation of individuals in the eastern bloc – a fact which explains Brandt's enormous popularity there.

1987-90

His resignation as party leader was another milestone in Brandt's life and, once the actual crisis was over, he was relieved to be freed from the pettier aspects of party work. But it was not to be quiet, immediate retirement. He put his own stamp on the Matheopoulos affair by deploring in several publications the many racist letters he had received and he used them to attack the poor state of human rights in the Federal Republic. In June 1987 he made his official farewell from the party at an extraordinary party congress in Bonn. As if to emphasize once more his political stance he took part in an impressive peace rally organized by the SPD on the day before, where he marched arm in arm with younger, 'left' party leaders of the next generation. His speech at the congress was 'vintage Brandt' ranging from a plea for charity for his past shortcomings to how resources saved in the process of disarmament could be transferred to the 'Third World'. On balance he could look back with satisfaction on what had been achieved under his party chairmanship: internal reforms – which although they had fallen short of many expectations had created new realities – and the policy of reconciliation (*Verständigungspolitik*), as a result of which the words 'Germany' and 'peace' were again (and for many Europeans: for the first time) synonymous. He defended his record as election winner, rather than loser: the SPD had lost elections recently because in a changed society the party had not been able to find new majorities; it had not been able to reach a large section of the young. Nevertheless, electoral defeat did not mean having to abandon the party's new found platform: 'A conviction is not wrong … because consent is not yet forthcoming … I could and cannot give the advice not to pursue the right concepts [just] because they are not attractive to the voters.' Finally, he said his farewell to the party and saw the historic perspective of the moment: with him the last chairman was leaving who had grown up in the old working class culture. But, characteristically, even now he was only going below, he was not leaving the ship. He would remain active in the party: 'everything else would be against my nature'. The conference gave him an emotional standing ovation and elected him Honorary Chairman for life, a position which had been especially created for him.

Brandt perhaps for the first time in his life now had time for writing, reading and travels of his own choosing rather than those imposed by official duty. He wrote his Memoirs and remained active in the Socialist International and in his own words, was entering the phase of the 'mild evening sun' of his life. Developments were to prove him very wrong.

The most remarkable feature about Brandt's Memoirs was initially the controversial way in which they were marketed. They were serialized first in September 1989 (for a handsome fee, it is rumoured) in the right wing Springer papers *Bild* and *Welt* which in the past had never tired of attacking Brandt's policies and person. (The publisher of the book was also on the right of the political spectrum.) Moreover, the contents also caused a stir, notably in party circles. For while Brandt was conciliatory towards his erstwhile competitor Schmidt ('the German European') he was relentless in his condemnation of Wehner who now bore all the blame for Brandt's resignation in 1974. The timing for this reckoning was unfortunate: Wehner lay dying and was in no way capable of standing up for himself. But Brandt's lack of generosity towards Wehner showed again how open the wound of his resignation still was. The Memoirs also revealed considerable disillusionment with the SPD which came through in Brandt's perception now of how tiring and basically hopeless the party leadership had been after the SPD's fall from power in 1982. This contrasted vividly with the impression he conveyed at the time of relief that the government had fallen at last and of optimism that after a short period of renewal the SPD would be back in power.

In 1988 and 1989 he travelled widely for the SI to Dacca, twice to Moscow and to Stockholm where at its 1989 Congress the SI adopted its 'Principles' (see above) and hammered out its responses to the new challenges in Eastern Europe, in addition to the organization's by now traditional preoccupation with disarmament. While endorsing the events in Eastern Europe the SI was aware of possible cruel reversals there. Aid must be provided, also via the socialist parties in the EC, to make such an eventuality less likely. The organizational problem, the status of the emerging socialist parties and the question of their membership in the SI would be solved in due course.

Meanwhile the process of political reform in Eastern Europe had spread to the GDR where it developed with particularly breathtaking speed with the resignation on 18 October of Erich Honecker who only weeks earlier had celebrated the 40th anniversary of the GDR's existence with all the display of a confident nation and in the presence of Gorbachev. However, daily, thousands of GDR citizens voted with their feet across the open borders of the GDR's neighbours; as in the other East European countries the Soviets did not interfere even when the population began to demand reforms in peaceful street demonstrations (Brandt with his excellent contacts with the Kremlin knew this in advance). Shortly afterwards the unthinkable happened: on 9 November 1989 the Wall in Berlin was breached for the first time in almost thirty years.

No West German politician could have been more affected by these events than Brandt. As Mayor of Berlin he had been unable to prevent the Wall's construction and much of his political life had been devoted to making life with it more bearable for the ordinary people. He now witnessed its opening with tears of joy. He was given a tumultuous reception by the Berlin population (Kohl was booed), and was greeted by enthusiastic crowds wherever he travelled in the GDR afterwards. In their eyes he, more than anyone, had cared about their fate. Brandt also coined the slogan which not only the SPD used to describe the momentous events: 'Now grows together what belongs together' – not only in Germany but in West and East Europe generally. With a united Germany increasingly a realistic option Brandt more and more came into his own: planning for a united Germany in a European Peace Order had preoccupied him throughout his political career, beginning during the years in exile. To see these plans come to fruition in some form was enormously exciting. An almost physical change came over Brandt who suddenly looked years younger despite the strain of numerous public engagements. For he had once more come back into the limelight; at no time since the hey-day of his Chancellorship had he enjoyed such popularity; indeed he together with the President, von Weizsacker, Foreign Secretary Genscher and Helmut Schmidt found the highest approval rating of any politician in Germany. He now had the satisfaction of hearing that erstwhile opponents of his *Ostpolitik* such as Kissinger, the former American Secretary of State, recognized their errors.

For the SPD he had become again the most important asset. He not only provided limitless publicity and allowed the party once more to bask in the successes of its past; he emerged as one of the few public figures who responded to the events in anything approaching a coherent way. It was therefore entirely logical that the SPD leadership should make Brandt its official spokesman on German affairs: party and ex-Chairman were now easily reconciled with each other; past tensions rapidly forgotten. This was demonstrated at the SPD's annual congress in December 1989 in Berlin. The congress coincided with Brandt's 76th birthday; his 'party', a public event, was a eulogy to the SPD's most outstanding personality.

His new role suited Brandt to the ground: free from the constraints of office he could speak with the authority of a lifetime in international affairs and, based on his reputation abroad, could help redress the balance in international public opinion against the utterances of some less circumspect leading German politicians. More-over, as contacts between East and West German politi-cians intensified he emerged as one of the few western politicians who showed tact and understanding for the difficult psychological position of the East Germans who were going through the profoundly confusing and humiliating experience of seeing their country crumbling before their eyes and who seemed to have little to offer to the prosperous and often overconfident West Germans in return. Brandt never showed the condescension or outright contempt with which other West German public figures treated their East German counterparts.

His position on the question of German unification had of course been clear for many years with his distinction between '*re*-unification' and 'unification'; he had always rejected all notions of recreating the German nation state within the borders of 1937 which the expression 're-unification' suggested: this had been the lie of the 1950s. The old Germany had vanished once and for all with Germany's military defeat at the end of the war. 'Unification' however signified the more modest objective of joining the two existing German states, the FRG and GDR, although in the past even its realization had seemed unlikely in view of the entrenched position of both blocs in Europe (hence Brandt's and the SPD's attempts to come to a modus vivendi with the SED). Now with a shift in Soviet policy a united Germany became a possibility although the precise form of this new German state would emerge in time. One scenario according to Brandt was the way via a joint treaty between the two states to a confederation similar to the German Confederation of the 19th century. When therefore at the end of November 1989 Chancellor Kohl announced his Ten Point Plan for German unity Brandt came out in its support. Kohl's speech – without prior consultation with the allies – but linking the 'German question' with Germany's Europe-wide commitments through membership in NATO and the CSCE (Helsinki) process was reminiscent of Brandt's first steps in his *Ostpolitik*. For both, Germany's future was essentially a German affair and the difference between what Brandt was able to do in the early 1970s and what Kohl could do in the 1990s reflected the changed position of the superpowers rather than traditional contradictions on policy between the two German parties. However, where Brandt differed fundamentally from Kohl was the question of the Polish borders which was ignored in the Ten Points. For Brandt Poland remained a special partner for the FRG; the immense suffering inflicted on the Polish people must never be forgotten. His standpoint on the Polish border question was therefore always clear; Chancellor Kohl's attempts in March 1990 to trade the recognition of the borders against Polish renunciation of claims to reparations from Germany was unthinkable for Brandt.

More than Kohl, Brandt was atuned to foreign perceptions of events in the FRG, and this explains his stance at the SPD's annual Congress in Berlin in December 1989. François Mitterand and Margaret Thatcher had expressed misgivings about German unification (albeit in different styles) and the Americans had remained non-committal, a position which was shared by the USSR although this hardly came as a surprise from the latter. However, the western powers had repeatedly paid lip service to German unification and their hesitations now seemed inappropriate to Brandt. In his speech, therefore, while placing emphasis on the process by which Europe was growing together again which gave renewed weight to the old continent and where Germany was only a sideshow he also put considerable stress on the 'German cause': the Germans had the right to solve their internal problems without interference from the outside; the German train need not wait until the European train had reached its destination. On the contrary, he appealed to the erstwhile occupation powers, not to expose the Germans excessively to 'diplomatic finesse' – this could lead to a possible nationalist backlash in the population(s). Moreover, the allies should not overlook that forty-five years after the end of the war the pattern of victors/vanquished no longer applied; they were dealing with second generation Germans. Young Germans wanted peace and freedom as did the young in other countries. 'However great the guilt of a nation, it cannot be paid for by an indefinite division.' Although Brandt scaled down his remarks immediately by stressing that no return to the old, pre-war nationalism was intended and that Europeans should not lose sight of the global perspectives, this was almost emotional patriotism. These remarks came as a surprise to his audience and were disconcerting at the time. However, they seemed to be aimed at different audiences simultaneously, such as those abroad. Inside the country they expressed Brandt's lifelong concern for 'Germany' as a whole as well as the attempt not to allow history to repeat itself and to leave the 'national' question again to the political Right as had happened under the Kaiser and in the Weimar Republic. This lack of 'national' commitment seemed to surface again now in younger members of the SPD and was illustrated by the speech of (the future Chancellor candidate) Oskar Lafontaine whose main concern was with the economic and social consequences of unification. Brandt, by contrast, never underestimated the emotional component contained in the question of Germany's future and with his fine antenna for public moods perceived growing popular support for a united 'Germany' which it was hoped could be turned into votes for the SPD. (There was also the – to the SPD – alarming fact that in January 1989 in Berlin the party had lost valuable votes to the right wing Republicans and they could thus be outflanked.)

A sizeable part of his speech was taken up with a reckoning with the now discredited East German SED – a particular problem for the SPD. The SPD leadership had been slow in grasping how a possible German unification might benefit the party. The previous course of *rapprochement* with the East German SED in order to achieve better contacts between the two German states had culminated in the publication of a joint SPD/SED position paper (*Streitkulturpapier*) in 1987 in which both sides declared that their systems should compete openly and that mutual criticism should not be taken as interfering in the internal affairs of the other side. However, when the SED came under increasing pressure for reform from the example of its neighbours and from the increasing emigration of its citizens, it withdrew from its cooperative stance and in September 1989 cancelled the visit to East Berlin of a high level SPD delegation. This was a well publicized embarrassment for the SPD, and the spokesman for the Bonn government rather nastily talked of the SPD's futile course of *Anbiederung* (chumminess) towards the GDR, an allusion to the Brandt/Bahr policy of *Annäherung* (*rapprochement*). Indeed, as political changes took place in the GDR, the absence of contacts between SPD and opposition groups in the GDR came under closer scrutiny, revealing considerable confusion in the SPD leadership which was made worse by its refusal to enter into a dialogue with the new SED leader Gregor Gysi where previously they had had numerous

The Shop Front.

contacts with Honecker. The great speed of events helped to distract public attention. Now, in Berlin, Brandt drew a firm line between SPD and SED: the party remembered well the way in which the SED had treated Social Democrats in the past. Moreover, there was an old all-German Social Democratic tradition which the party could go back to. Indeed it was on this basis that a great deal of material help was given to the East German SDP which had been founded illegally on 7 October – before Honecker's fall and against the advice of the SPD West. Members of the SDP took part in SPD events, received advice on tactics and organization (and vital pieces of equipment such as photocopiers etc.) from the SPD and, once free travel was possible to the east, members of the west-SPD, including Brandt, addressed East German meetings together with members of the east-SPD. This cooperation culminated in January 1990 in an open confederation between the two parties, with the SDP adopting the traditional name SPD. In February 1990 Brandt also became Honorary chairman of the GDR SDP and immediately used its new authority to exhort his East German audiences to perservere in their country and help with its reconstruction.

During this period Brandt's star seemed to be rising inexorably. Discussion about the way in which Germany could be unified focused increasingly on the use of Article 146 of the West German Basic Law according to which an all-German Constitutional Council would work out a new constitution. Brandt was the main candidate to chair such a Council. At the same time he tried to use his regained popularity to draw attention to the worsening plight of the Third World which he felt should not be forgotten in the flurry of European and German enthusiasms. In January 1990 he chaired a meeting of his North-South Commission in Bonn which pledged new initiatives because, since the publication of the Brandt Report, the situation of the world's poorest countries had not only not improved but had deteriorated drastically. Now, when the process of disarmament placed more resources at the disposal of national governments Brandt called for a renewed effort to be made to revive the North-South dialogue and to achieve the necessary transfer of resources for the fight against hunger and disease and against the dangers to the environment. This was 'The Challenge of the 1990s' (the motto of the conference). By the autumn of 1990 an Action Programme was to be developed in which the results of the Brandt, Palme and Brundtland Commissions, as well as that of the South Commission headed by Julius Nyerere would be pooled and which would be presented to the world's governments, to the UN and to other international organizations. The repetition of the Cancun summit would take place at the beginning of 1991, exactly ten years after the failure of Cancun I. Brandt remained as optimistic as ever. 'Now we begin again, in the hope of advancing a little more.'[5]

In Germany too, developments seemed to be working in Brandt's and the SPD's favour. By February 1990, once Gorbachev had dropped his reservations, German unification, in Brandt's view, was a foregone conclusion, although formidable practical problems remained. In the event, these problems proved unexpectedly damaging to the SPD as the situation in the GDR deteriorated rapidly with over 50,000 East Germans leaving their country in January 1990 alone. It seemed that neither East nor West Germany's government was prepared to take decisive action: the East Germans dragged their feet over real political and economic reforms and the West Germans were less than generous with aid to the, still, communist regime. A more legitimate East German government could emerge only after elections there and these had to be moved forward from May to 18 March 1990.

The campaign for the first democratic election in the GDR since 1932 was fought less by East German activists

than by the direct involvement of the West German
parties who thought that the result there would be a
forerunner of the West German vote in December 1990.
Brandt had deplored this danger already in November
1989 and had unsuccessfully called for the setting up of a
national coalition which would provide an above-party-
platform for the nation's most complicated problems. He,
together with President von Weizsäcker and Foreign
Secretary Genscher continued to take up this above-party
stance during the next months. (According to opinion
polls in February 1990[6] their standing in the population
was considerably higher than that of Chancellor Kohl.)
Although Brandt addressed numerous pre-election meetings throughout the GDR he never quite abandoned this,
appealing to the East Germans to 'make less haste' over
unification and not to give up their traditions and
achievements too quickly. However, the SPD's campaign
was hampered by the obvious division between the two
leading SPD campaigners. Whereas Brandt never left
national unification as such in doubt, Lafontaine was
uneasy on this issue and his speeches against unlimited
East German immigration into the FRG during the election campaign in the Saarland in January 1990, to the
East Germans, smacked of a lack of solidarity. Moreover,
the East German SPD fought a lacklustre campaign partly
because of a lack of experience but partly also because it
was over-confident of victory. The party's prospects
appeared very good: of all East German parties the SPD
alone had had strong direct links with a party in the west
and common roots with it in a party predating the
communist dictatorship. A vote of 52 per cent for the
SPD was being predicted in January 1990. Moreover, the
south of the GDR had been traditionally 'left' so that
there was hope among the SPD (West) that in future the
electoral balance in the west would shift in their favour
and revitalize its flagging electoral fortunes. As the elections approached they were seen more and more as a

repetition of those in 1949 when fundamental choices had been made. Then Democratic Socialism had been defeated and it seemed to Brandt that now, via East Germany, it had another chance. This explained his tireless campaigning activities. He addressed huge crowds but it was significant that these became smaller as the elections approached.

This was due mainly to the increasingly important personal role of Chancellor Kohl in the campaign who saw in quick unification the best way of overcoming hesitations among Germany's allies and who believed that an SPD victory in the GDR would not only delay unification dangerously, it would also have long-term consequences for the FRG. He therefore intervened actively and more or less forced the reluctant East German 'bourgeois' politicians (the former official GDR-CDU, and two new groups, Democratic Awakening and the more conservative German Social Union) into a coalition, the Alliance for Germany, which then received generous aid from the west. Kohl himself toured the GDR and for the first time in his political career enjoyed mass audiences who were attracted by his message: speedy unification through the joining of the individual states of the GDR to the FRG on the basis of Article 23 of the Basic Law and the introduction of the DM in the GDR (at an amazing exchange rate of 1:1) and with it the prospect of western prosperity. The SPD by contrast increasingly lost its attractiveness: voters who wanted 'unity now' moved to the Alliance and those who were uncertain about unification drifted to the communist PDS.

The drama of the elections was reflected in a poll of 93.2 per cent. The result, with 48 per cent for Kohl's Alliance, 22 per cent for the SPD and 16 per cent for the PDS, was devastating not only for the SPD but also for opinion pollsters who with their total miscalculations had found their 'Waterloo'.[7] It emerged that larger sections of the population than expected had been won over by the hope that Kohl would provide speedy economic recovery. Moreover, CDU propaganda was highly effec-

tive, equating SPD with SED (both were socialists), and
Brandt was attacked in familiar style by the publicizing of
past love affairs which he had allegedly had with two well
known German film stars. However although Brandt's
personal standing among East Germans remained high,
he had no power and it was difficult to see how an SPD-
led East German government could gain from Bonn the
necessary concessions which the East German population
were expecting. This explains the overwhelming vote for
the Alliance particularly in working class areas of the
south of the GDR where scores of workers opted for
better wages and working conditions which only the
government party in Bonn could deliver. In a reversal of
'normal' voting behaviour the CDU polled well over 50
per cent of the vote in the big cities (except in Berlin)
but did significantly less well in rural areas. These elections therefore may well say little about long-term political allegiances in the GDR although Brandt conceded
that his attempt to revive the 'common roots' with the
workers in the GDR had failed and that 'in 57 years something more than a new party had grown in the GDR'.[8]

Brandt was deeply affected by this outcome. He was
disgusted by yet another personal smear campaign
against him, and by the equation of SPD with SED ('I shall
never forgive them for this'). Not surprisingly Brandt felt
that the CDU had 'bought' the votes of the East Germans.[9]
His disappointment showed in another bout of melancholy
when after the elections he described his life as having
consisted of 'more reversals than successes'; the most recent
defeat was seen as yet another episode in a life with a fair
share of painful failures. However, he also felt that 'in the
last analysis we have persevered after all;[10] in the situation
after the election this meant that the SPD-East, unlike its
counterpart in the west in 1949, did not opt for 'splendid
isolation' but entered the GDR coalition government.
Brandt who was the 'foster father' of the East German SPD
leadership was instrumental in bringing about this decision.

Conclusion

The life of Willy Brandt has the quality of a fairy tale. This applies to the 'rags to riches' aspect of the rise of a poor, illegitimate working class lad to become Chancellor of the Federal Republic of Germany and the winner of the Nobel Peace Prize. It also seems to appear in the later part of his life, when after the comparative failure of the North-South Commission and his resignation from the SPD leadership in controversy, Brandt's earlier work suddenly came to unexpected fruition with Gorbachev's change of course in Eastern Europe which led to the realization of Brandt's most cherished objectives. From the peaceful existence of semi-retirement Brandt was catapulted into the heights of public acclaim. More than ever he is revealed as a 'Maker of the 20th Century'.

Brandt was a man of great energy and strong personal ambition who from an early age wanted to succeed even in situations where he had no realistic chance of winning. He was a young man in a hurry and even later he was driven on to succeed – a sentiment which left him to some extent after the crisis in 1965, when a second attempt to become Chancellor had ended in resounding failure. However, it seemed to reappear in 1969 when observers commented on his unusual decisiveness; after his resignation from office in 1974 in his determination to build a new career for himself; and after 1982 in his attempt to change the SPD and to continue to play an international role.

It is easy to see the motives for this in Brandt's personal history and perhaps also in the traditional working class emphasis on self-improvement which his mother and grandfather so aptly illustrate. However, in Brandt this comes together with an unusual ability to adapt to new circumstances and the combinations of determination and adaptability proved one of his strongest assets. He displayed it early on in exile where unlike many of his compatriots he quickly settled into a new life, learning not only Norwegian but a score of other foreign languages as well. This *Lernfähigkeit* (ability to learn) never left him throughout his life which explains the breadth of his vision and also the development of the, to many observers, alarming change of his political ideas. This was indeed remarkable; already in exile he was accused of lacking commitment to 'principle' because he was abandoning his early adherence to what had become a sectarian blend of socialism in favour of a reformist Social Democracy of the Scandinavian type. In the late 1940s he showed right-wing leanings when fighting with Reuter in Berlin against the communist threat. In the 1950s and 60s he opened the sessions of the Berlin City Council with the solemn vow to work towards German reunification; and he supported the policies of the USA even in Vietnam because their defeat would undermine the 'policy of strength' towards the USSR in Europe. After the construction of the Berlin Wall he adapted to a change in international politics (illustrated by the American/Soviet rapprochement after the Cuban Missile Crisis) and gradually moved towards rapprochement with the Soviets with the policy of 'small steps'; this culminated in *Ostpolitik* with a cautious distancing from the USA in favour of a greater freedom of action for Europe and for West Germany in it. This European perspective was dramatically widened as a result of

Conclusion

his work for the North–South Commission which alerted him to the global challenge of the fundamental problems of the Third World such as mass starvation and persistent under development. These put the by now entrenched East–West conflict into perspective; together with the experiences gained in the SI it also changed his views of the USA and the western industrialised world generally. This in turn helps to explain his more 'left' stance in his later life on questions such as disarmament, nuclear power and the environment.

However, it seems that on certain matters Brandt's views did not change. From his days in exile he was preoccupied with the position of Europe in the world and that of Germany in it. For him the 'Europeanization of Germany' was essential for peace and stability in Europe and this in turn would help developments in the 'German Question'. (To this one must add the Third World in his later life.) A second constant was his continued commitment to democratic socialism and its work for social justice, equality of opportunity and freedom. Within these broad confines Brandt remained open to new challenges.

It was this looking forward to new developments and the critical questioning of the present which endeared him to the young. But this was essentially an intellectual approach to politics rather than an approach based on the aspiration to and exercise of power. It reflected on and examined issues. Brandt remained the highly articulate journalist who loved the formulation of new ideas to the extent that whenever he could, he wrote his own speeches using the material of his staff as a basis. He disliked drafts where there was no opportunity for his own improvements and made meticulous corrections. However, although he took Rathenau, the Foreign Secretary of the Weimar Republic, the 'intellectual in politics', as one of his models Brandt was not really an intellectual in the Rathenau mould. Instead he was more a visionary or a synthesizer of ideas. He saw the main achievement of *Ostpolitik* in the new perspectives which had been opened up, in the way in which the atmosphere had been improved. It is noteworthy that he approached the work of the North-South Commission in the same way; he wanted to repeat what he had done in *Ostpolitik*, create a new public awareness, alert public opinion to the disasters in the Third World and by thus changing the perspective bring about new approaches. His work as President of the Socialist International consists in precisely this function. On the other hand this approach to politics is less well suited to day-to-day administration and this helps explain his resignation in 1974: the vision of *Ostpolitik* was becoming reality, the reforms were under way. Brandt's real job seemed done. This also comes through in the North-South Commission where he certainly succeeded in gaining world-wide publicity (and where he has since worked tirelessly to keep the Third World on the international agenda). However, he did not gain much of direct benefit for the Third World, admittedly an almost impossible task, because the report was perhaps not sufficiently 'down-to-earth' or orientated towards the requirements of actual development work to bring even modest progress. On the other hand, it was this very ability to look at known facts from different perspectives and to improve the atmosphere in which others would work which ultimately produced results where other, more 'realistic' approaches would have made no impact. Without Brandt's vision there would have been no *Ostpolitik*.

By the same token he rarely gave the impression of being particularly hungry for power for its own sake, except perhaps in his early days in Berlin, and this distinguishes him clearly from other politicians such as Schmidt. This may be the key to an understanding of Brandt's conduct during the final crisis which led to Schmidt's fall. A point seemed to have been reached where the pursuit of power for its own sake was not worth undertaking (although using the Brandtian device of the 'on the one hand – but on the other' we must add that other factors also contributed to the outcome). This is also born out by the way Brandt conducted committees or even cabinets where he failed to impose his authority, hoping for a consensus to emerge to the extent that efficiency was at times affected. It is also reflected in his dislike of confrontation both on a larger scale in parliament (he was never leader of the SPD in the *Bundestag*) or when dealing with Wehner, or with his staff where he was often unable to sack inefficient individuals with at times disastrous consequences (e.g. in the Chancellery after 1972, Guillaume and later in the SI). There was, for a politician, an unusual soft centre to him which was vulnerable to criticism and which could easily take offence; he was on the other hand quite able to hit out at others and sometimes retaliated years after the event such as when as party leader, he did not attend parliament when Schmidt gave his final address in September 1986.

On the other hand this vulnerability may also explain his moods and depressions, which were often made worse by his 'swinging' lifestyle. Until recently he came across as a man of great strengths and weaknesses which polarized the public into those who either loved or hated him; indifference towards him was rare. Many saw and see as his main strength his concern for ordinary people; indeed even at the time of his SAP membership he reminded his colleagues that most people were moved less by '-isms' than by food, drink, canaries and other good things in life. This translated later into a policy of 'small steps', of improvements to the day-to-day life of the people of Berlin and the GDR. He also used his travels abroad to intercede with the authorities of his host countries on behalf of countless politically persecuted individuals. On a different level this empathy with ordinary people made him one of the most effective public speakers in German history, he has just been made 'Speaker of the Year' for 1989. Some observers believe that not since Hitler have mass meetings been so moved by an individual politician of such charisma.

Brandt thus emerges as a highly complex personality. His impact on German public life has been profound, not only in the kind of policies he pursued or attempted but also in other, indirect ways. With the change of government in 1969 the normal working of the political system was assured. After Brandt and thirteen years of SPD-led government West German society is more open and more relaxed about its past, more modern and, the Decree on Extremists in Public Service notwithstanding, a more tolerant and confident society. It is more conscious of environmental and Third World problems than other comparable states. In international affairs Brandt's influence has been even more marked. From a passive player in international affairs, West Germany under Brandt gained a freedom of action which ultimately turned it into one of the prime movers of détente. It has helped to bring about momentous changes in the centre of Europe. Brandt's greatest monument would be for the Third World ultimately to share the benefit.

References

Chapter 1

1. The account of Brandt's youth and exile is based on W. Brandt, *My Road to Berlin*, Peter Davies, London, 1960, and on W. Brandt, *Links und Frei, Mein Weg 1930–1950*, Hoffman und Campe, Hamburg, 1982. Quotations are from these books unless otherwise stated.
2. E. Lorenz, Willy Brandt in *Norwegen, Die Jahre des Exils 1933–1940*, Neuer Malik Verlag, Kiel, 1989, p. 76 *passim*.
3. Lorenz, p. 220.
4. Brandt, Links und Frei, p. 194.
5. P. Koch, Willy Brandt. *Eine politische Biographie*, Ullstein, Frankfurt, 1988, p. 120 *passim*.
6. Koch, p. 125.

Chapter 2

1. W. Brandt, Draussen, *Schriften während der Emigration*, Dietz, München, 1966, p. 51 Letter to J. Walcher 14 August 1945.

2. Draussen, p. 344.
3. Draussen, p. 354 Letter to E. Lange 7 November 1947.
4. Willy Brandt, Reports from Berlin, No. 15/26 February 1948. In: Archiv der Friedrich Ebert Stiftung (FES), Bonn. Bestand Schumacher J 79 I. Berlin Parteivorstand Sekretariat 2, January 1948–February 1949.
5. C. Stern, Willy Brandt in *Selbstzeugnissen und Bilddokumenten*, Rororo Reinbek 1975, p. 150
6. H.G. Lehmann, *In Acht und Bann, Politische Emigration*, NS-Ausbürgerung und Wiedergutmachung am Beispiel Willy Brandts, C.H. Beck, München, 1976, p. 259 *passim* for the following.
7. Lehmann, p. 251.
8. Lehmann, p. 259.
9. K. Hildebrand, *Von Ehrhard zur Grossen Koalition 1963–1969*. (Geschichte der Bundesrepublik Deutschland, IV) DVA/Brockhaus, Stuttgart/Mannheim, 1984, p. 147.
10. Lehmann, p. 252 quoting 'Bild' 23 November 1964.
11. C. Stern, p. 75.

Chapter 3

1. Hildebrand, p. 204.
2. Hildebrand, p. 272 *passim* for the following.
3. Willy Brandt, *Reden und Interviews 1968–69*, Presse und Informations amt der Bundestegierung, Bonn, 1969, p. 102.
4. H. Schreiber/F. Sommer, Gustav Heinemann, *Bundespräsident*, Frankfurt, 1969, p. 49.
5. A. Baring, *Machtwechsel, Die Ära Brandt-Scheel*, DVA, Stuttgart, 1982, p. 132.

Chapter 4

1. W.Jäger, 'Die Innenpolitik der sozialliberalen Koalition

1969–1974'. in: *Die Republik im Wandel.* (Geschichte der Bundesrepublik Deutschland, vol. V/I) DVA/ Brockhaus, Stuttgart/Mannheim, 1986, p. 26 for the following.

2. Koch, p. 357.
3. P. Borowsky, Deutschland 1970–1976, Facketräger Verlag, Hannover, 1983, p. 56.
4. 'Die Zeit' 4.2.1972.
5. Willy Brandt, *Über den Tag hinaus.* Eine Zwischenbilanz, Hoffman und Campe, Hamburg, 1974, p. 39.
6. Jäger, p. 87.
7. Jäger, p. 115 for the following.
8. Brandt, Über den Tag hinaus, p. 181.

Chapter 5

1. 'Die Zeit' 7.4.1989.
2. Jahrbuch der SPD, 1970–1972, p. 305.
3. G. Braunthal, *The West German Social Democrats 1969–1982, Profile of a Party in Power*, Westview Press, Boulder/Colorado, 1983, p. 142.
4. W. Link, 'Aussen-und Deutschlandpolitik der Ära Schmidt' 1974–1982, in: *Republik im Wandel 1974–1982*, Die Ära Schmidt. (Geschichte der Bundersrepublik Deutschland, vol. V/2) DVA/Brockhaus Stuttgart/Mannheim, 1987, p. 324.
5. Willy Brandt Interview WDF 'Momente' 23 October 1979. In: Archiv FES, Deponat Willy Brandt, Publikationen 0537.
6. 'Neue Gesellschaft' 12/1981.
7. Willy Brandt Interview Radio Beromünster, 27 November 1976. As in (5), 245.
8. 'Die Zeit' 20 November 1980.
9. Willy Brandt, Opening Speech at first session of the North-South Commission, 9 December 1977, as in (5), 248.
10. Willy Brandt, *World Armament and World Hunger, A*

Call for Action, Gollancz, London, 1986, p. 104.
11. Willy Brandt, Interview 'Der Überblick', 18 March 1984, as in(5), 23 March–31 March 1984.
12. Archiv FES, Deponat Willy Brandt, ICIDI 1977–1985.

Chapter 6

1. Link as in (chp.5. ref 4), p. 24.
2. J. Derbyshire, *Politics in West Germany*, W. & R. Chambers, London, 1987, p. 69.
3. 'Der Spiegel' 30 March 1987.
4. 'Der Spiegel'.
5. 'Das Parlament' 24 January 1990.
6. 'Die Zeit' 16 March 1990.
7. 'Der Spiegel' 19 March 1990.
8. 'Die Zeit' 23 March 1990.
9. Willy Brandt, Interview BBC TV 18 March 1990.
10. 'Die Zeit' 23 March 1990.

Select Bibliography

Brandt has written extensively about his political career, his objectives and ideas. The most important volumes of personal recollections in English are:

My Road to Berlin, Peter Davies, London, 1960.
In Exile, Essays, Reflections and Letters 1933–1947, Oswald Wolff, London, 1971.
People and Politics, William Collins Sons & Co. Ltd. London, 1978.

Brandt's most recent volume of memoirs is not yet available in English:

Willy Brandt, *Erinnerungen*, Propyläen, Frankfurt/Zürich, 1989.

The findings of the North-South Commission were published in two reports:

The Independent Commission on International Development Issues,
North-South: a Programme for Survival, Pan, London, 1980.

Common Crisis, North-South: Co-operation for World Recovery, Pan, London, 1983.

A summary of Brandt's views on the issues raised can be found in:

Willy Brandt, *World Armament and World Hunger, A Call for Action*. Gollancz, London, 1986.

There are surprisingly few satisfactory biographies of Willy Brandt; in English they were written during or immediately after Brandt's Chancellorship. The most informative is:

T. Prittie, *Willy Brandt*, London, 1974.

In German the most balanced account is still:

C. Stern, *Willy Brandt in Selbstzeugnissen und Bilddokumenten*, Rororo, Reinbek, 1975.

The two most recent books are either too sympathetic to Brandt, such as:

G. Hoffmann, Willy Brandt — *Porträt eines Aufklärers aus Deutschland*, Rororo, Reinbeck, 1988

or unfair to Brandt such as:

G. Koch, *Willy Brandt, Eine politische Biographie*, Ullstein, Frankfurt, 1988.

The best general background information on the FRG is provided by:

G. Kloss, *West Germany, An Introduction*, Second Edition, Macmillan, London, 1990.

Select Bibliography

For the political system see:

G. Smith, *Democracy in Western Germany, Parties and Politics in the Federal Republic*, 3rd edition, Heinemann, London, 1987

or

C.C. Schweitzer a.o. (eds), *Politics and Government in the Federal Republic of Germany, Basic Documents*, Berg, Lemington Spa, 1984.

For a more detailed historical background see:

W. Carr, *A History of Germany 1815–1985*, E. Arnold, London, 1987

and

G. Craig, *Germany 1866 to 1945*, Oxford University Press, Oxford, 1981.

There is also an excellent general analysis of the German 'national character' in:

G. Craig, *The Germans*, Pelican Books, Harmondsworth, 1984.

Index

Index

Index

Index

Index

Ulbricht, Walter, 38, 79, 80
Ulbricht Doctrine, 63
United Nations, 76, 81, 114, 121
    International Development
        Agency, 124, 127

Vansittart, Lord, 21
Versailles, Peace Treaty, 1, 28, 62
Vietnam, 59, 139, 160
Vogel, Hans Jochen, 129
Volksbote, 8–9, 10

Warsaw Pact, 59, 63
Warsaw Treaty, 77–9

Wehner, Herbert, 42, 48, 50, 55–7,
    72, 85, 91, 99, 101, 105, 112,
    129, 147, 163
Weimar Republic, 1, 7, 23, 62
Weizsacker, President von, 149,
    156
Weltbuhne, 16
Westpolitik, 91
World Bank, 120, 121

Yom Kippur War, 98
Youth International, 17
Young Socialists, 85
youth protests, 2